A great marriage is the product of great partnership—something Wil and Autumn Lake exemplify. *Togetherness* will position you to experience relationships the way God intended. Read this book if you're ready to transform your perception of what it looks like to do life with your spouse.

-John Bevere - Messenger International
Minister and Best-Selling Author

I have had the privilege of working alongside Wil and Autumn Lake for many years now as they have served as campus pastors and marriage ministry pastors of our local church. Our journey as friends and co-pastors has allowed me to see the authenticity of this powerful message they are now bringing to couples everywhere. This content has been time-tested in the furnace of real life and will undoubtedly make your marriage stronger!

Dave Patterson, Lead Pastor-
The Father's House, Vacaville CA

I have been a longtime friend of Wil Lake. He and his wife, Autumn, were on my staff as Pastors early on in their marriage. They have always exemplified the love and respect a married couple should have and grow with all the days of their marriage. Here is a walk through the real issues covered in a biblical way, where any and all married couples will find encouragement and pathways to follow.

Dr. Frank Damazio, Lead Pastor –
City Bible Church, Portland OR
Author of *The Making of a Leader*, *Strategic Church* and *Life Changing Leadership*.

Sometimes when you hear about a book you immediately know that the topic of the book is the perfect topic for that author. That's how I felt when I heard that Wil Lake had written this book. Not only is it a much needed resource for couples, but it's written in a way that only experience and insight can convey. I highly recommend *Togetherness* for couples at all stages of life and relationship.

Kevin Gerald, Lead Pastor –
Champions Centre, Tacoma WA
Author of *Good Things* and *Mind Monsters*.

Togetherness is much more than a book; it is a marriage manual to help couples build a strong marriage together. A lasting marriage does not just happen; it takes 2 people working together. The Lakes have modeled that kind of marriage and have written Togetherness to help others achieve the same thing.

Benny Perez, Lead Pastor - The Church LV
Best Selling Author of *More: Discovering The
God of More When Life Gives You Less*

Becky & I have known Wil Lake for over 25 years and throughout the years, Wil and his wife, Autumn, have modeled what a beautiful, healthy, joyful, whole marriage and family is. This book will help many find deep fulfillment in their homes and marriage! A must read!

Jude Fouquier, Lead Pastor - The City Church Ventura

Wil Lake's *Togetherness* provides a blueprint for experiencing God's best in marriage. This book is a treasure that will help you look at partnership in a brand-new way. This book is a treasure that will help you look at partnership in a brand-new way. You will discover God's special destiny for your marriage and see that your future together is bright with promise.

Roger Crawford, author of *How High Can You Bounce*,
Think Again and *Playing from The Heart*.

TOGETHERNESS

Couples Living Life Better Together

— WIL LAKE —

WESTBOW
PRESS®
A DIVISION OF THOMAS NELSON
& ZONDERVAN

WestBow Press books may be ordered through booksellers or by contacting:

WestBow Press
A Division of Thomas Nelson & Zondervan
1663 Liberty Drive
Bloomington, IN 47403
www.westbowpress.com
1 (866) 928-1240

Because of the dynamic nature of the Internet, any web addresses or
links contained in this book may have changed since publication and
may no longer be valid. The views expressed in this work are solely those
of the author and do not necessarily reflect the views of the publisher,
and the publisher hereby disclaims any responsibility for them.

Any people depicted in stock imagery provided by Thinkstock are models,
and such images are being used for illustrative purposes only.
Certain stock imagery © Thinkstock.

ISBN: 978-1-5127-4970-0 (sc)
ISBN: 978-1-5127-4971-7 (hc)
ISBN: 978-1-5127-4969-4 (e)

Library of Congress Control Number: 2016911549

Print information available on the last page.

WestBow Press rev. date: 09/08/2016

Contents

Acknowledgments vii

Introduction ix

Part One: Coming Together

Chapter 1: Designed for Togetherness 1

Chapter 2: Cultural View of Marriage 8

Chapter 3: God's View of Marriage 20

Part Two: Talking Together

Chapter 4: Meaningful Conversation 33

Chapter 5: Connected Conversation 38

Chapter 6: Intimate Conversation 50

Part Three: Deciding Together

Chapter 7: That Little Thing Called Unity 59

Chapter 8: Steps to Deciding Together 63

Part Four: Fighting Together

Chapter 9: The Cause of Conflict in Marriage 73

Chapter 10: How We Hurt Each Other when We Fight 78

Chapter 11: How to Fight Together and Win 83

Part Five: Sleeping Together

Chapter 12: Sex in Today's Culture 93
Chapter 13: Sex in God's Eyes...103
Chapter 14: Men—What Your Wife Wants.........................107
Chapter 15: Women—What Your Husband Wants 112

Part Six: Parenting Together

Chapter 16: The Incredibleness of Parenting Together.........125
Chapter 17: The Main Things...130
Chapter 18: The Wins..142
Chapter 19: The Tools...163

Part Seven: Staying Together

Chapter 20: Back from the Brink 179

Endnotes 191

Acknowledgments

To my amazing wife, Autumn, who has been the sole recipient of my togetherness for over thirty years: thank you for saying yes, thank you for staying during the tough times, and thank you for your undying love.

To Rachel, Christina, Joshua, and Alyssa: you are the gift that keeps on giving. It's an honor to be your father. You continue to bring joy to my life.

To Mom and Dad: this book would never have been written without your influence and example in my life of a couple who enjoys togetherness in marriage.

To the church I serve in: The Father's House, the greatest church with the best people on earth: it's a pleasure to serve on such a great team, headed by our lead pastor, Dave Patterson.

To the team at WestBow Press: Thank you for your assistance, your encouragement, and your expertise in helping get this book published.

Finally, to the countless couples who over the years allowed me to help, encourage, and counsel them: this book is a result of not only what I was able to teach you but what you taught me. I'm grateful.

Introduction

Let's start this journey of togetherness with a brief medical lesson about a heart disease that each of us would like to suffer from someday, *takotsubo cardiomyopathy*. This condition is also known as *broken heart syndrome* and is common within the physical body of a spouse who has just lost a loved one to whom they have been married for many years. Takotsubo cardiomyopathy is a physical response to an emotional heartbreak. It's been known to cause the stoppage of a beating heart within hours of the passing of a loved spouse. It's also known as the widowhood effect[1].

In July of 2015, in San Diego, California, Alexander Toczko was bedridden from a broken hip he'd suffered in a fall. He was ninety-six years old. His wife of seventy-five years, Jeanette, ninety-five years old, stayed by his side to help him as much as she could. Alexander and Jeanette had met each other when they were eight years old. Talk about love at first sight. They were wed in 1942. Alexander was a Navy veteran of WWII. After he broke his hip, Alexander asked hospice staff to set up a bed for the both him and Jeanette. They celebrated their seventy-fifth anniversary in that bed. And in that same bed, they would both pass from this life within twenty-four hours of each other. Their daughter, Aimee Toczko-Cushman, said, "Their hearts beat as one from as long as I can remember. He died in her arms, which is exactly what he wanted. She hugged him, and she said, 'See, this is what you wanted. You died in my arms, and I love you. I love you. Wait for me; I'll be there soon.'"[2] Within a few hours, she was.

(Wipe your eyes here).

There are many stories like this, stories of couples who marry, experience togetherness, and die still madly in love with the same person they married so many years ago. I personally want to live out Alexander and Jeanette's story. I want to stay together with my wife, Autumn, for seventy-five years, have her take her last breath in my arms, and then catch a bad case of takotsubo cardiomyopathy and join her, continuing our togetherness in heaven. A guy can dream, can't he?

This book is written for married couples who are committed to taking their togetherness experience in marriage to the limits of "death do us part." I want this book to inspire you and give you practical principles on how you can come together, live together, and stay together in a marriage full of fun, excitement, adventure, and victories over the challenges that will come your way.

Each section of *Togetherness* has multiple chapters designed to give you focus on one particular part of your togetherness experience, from helping you understand God's design for marriage, to talking, deciding, fighting, sleeping, parenting and, finally, staying together. Open your minds and your hearts as you read, and ask God to help you see the areas you need to work on. And most of all, open up to each other and discuss what you are learning as you make your way through each chapter and what you want/need to add or subtract from your togetherness journey. And let me add this final thought: do it together!

Part One

Coming Together

Chapter 1

Designed for Togetherness

Ketchup and mustard. Salt and pepper. Mickey and Minnie. Peanut butter and jelly. Milk and cookies. Dogs and cats. Err … wait a minute. Maybe not dogs and cats. Cats shouldn't be together with anything or anybody, but I digress. Most things were meant to be together. God made it that way. He made us that way. We were created by God to be together with other people to share life with. We were "woven together" in our mother's womb (Psalm 139:15). For those of you new to class, this was the result of your birth parents "getting together," if you know what I mean (we'll be talking about this in a later chapter called Sleeping Together). We were born into a family. All of us have parents, most of us have siblings, and hopefully you have friends who you consider family.

As we grew up, families tended to stretch beyond those with whom we lived in the same house. Aunts and uncles, cousins, and grandparents made up a circle of togetherness that surrounded us. Birthdays and holidays were big events, with family members and close friends celebrating together. It's also true that each family situation is different. Maybe you grew up with a single parent or never knew extended family. My birth mom was an unwed teenager who gave me up for adoption as an infant. A wonderful couple adopted me and became my parents. My sister is also adopted. So our blood doesn't match, but our bond of love does. I never met my birth parents, but I was able to experience true togetherness in my adopted family.

Our childhood consisted of teachers, coaches, bosses, and pastors. We also had certain close friends whose parents treated us like their own kids. They fed us, allowed us to spend the night at their homes, and even yelled at us as they would their own kid when we deserved it. What's great about togetherness is that people reach out, take others in, and include them in their lives. Togetherness.

This book is written to a specific part of the togetherness experience—the strongest, most intimate, and enduring relationship you have on earth. The person you are married to. Your husband. Your wife. Your covenant partner. The one whose hand you held and whose eyes you looked into when you made a verbal covenant of commitment in front of God and witnesses: "Until death do us part."

Two People Coming Together in Relationship Is a Natural Part of Life

The desire to be with someone is bestowed upon our hearts by God. So we have to look back at the beginning, creation, to see how marriage started and how togetherness was experienced with the first humans, Adam and Eve.

We know that God created Adam out of the dust of the earth and Eve out of Adam's rib. A man and a woman. Both made in God's image. Both able to love God and to love each other. What's interesting about Adam is that as he looked around creation before Eve came along, he liked what he saw and was totally satisfied. Every day of creation was a beautiful, mind-blowing masterpiece—a magnum opus of creative splendor backed by intricate science that can never be totally explained nor understood by the human mind. And Adam was there experiencing it firsthand. The Bible records that creation days one through five were days of extravagant creativity by God. God fashioned each element of creation to glorify himself, with man being the ultimate in creative magnificence as an independent, intelligent, free-willed being able to communicate with God and make decisions on his own. Despite all of this, God knew something was still missing in Adam's life, even though Adam himself wasn't aware of it. Now, don't misunderstand; Adam was totally whole as a person. God filled every area of his life. Like Adam, we are totally complete when we surrender our lives to God. God is the source of everything we need. Yet God has instilled in each of us a desire for human connection and relationship in addition to our spiritual relationship with him. In this book, I am calling the desire for human connection *togetherness*. What was missing in Adam's life was someone he could experience togetherness with. Even though Adam didn't know it at the time, he needed someone to help him fulfill the responsibilities of tending the garden and watching over God's creation. God was enough for Adam, but Adam wasn't enough for God. God wanted Adam to have someone to have and to hold, to love and cherish, and to enjoy human life with—not to mention having a partner with whom to bear children to populate this beautiful planet, so they could worship and serve God while taking dominion over the earth. Thus God put Adam under spiritual anesthesia, removed a rib from his side, and formed a woman. She became Adam's togetherness partner, and his life was changed forever.

> The Lord God said, "It is not good for the man to be alone. I will make a helper suitable for him."

Now the Lord God had formed out of the ground all the wild animals and all the birds in the sky. He brought them to the man to see what he would name them; and whatever the man called each living creature, that was its name. So the man gave names to all the livestock, the birds in the sky and all the wild animals.

But for Adam no suitable helper was found. So the Lord God caused the man to fall into a deep sleep; and while he was sleeping, he took one of the man's ribs and then closed up the place with flesh. Then the Lord God made a woman from the rib he had taken out of the man, and he brought her to the man.

The man said, "This is now bone of my bones and flesh of my flesh; she shall be called 'woman,' for she was taken out of man."

That is why a man leaves his father and mother and is united to his wife, and they become one flesh. (Genesis 2:18–24 NIV).

When God brought Eve to Adam, Adam experienced emotion that he had never felt before. Adam was love-struck. The animals in the Garden of Eden were cute, soft, and fuzzy (okay, some were prickly, ugly, and scary), but nothing compared to what he saw when Eve came into view. Here was someone like him. *Together* they could communicate, *together* they could connect emotionally, and *together* they could live out their dreams. And let's not forget Eve's perspective. She had that same rapturous moment. As Adam came into view and she saw him for the first time, her heart filled with emotion, passion, and excitement. She watched him move toward her, felt him take her into his arms, and heard him express the most romantic thought ever in human history—that they were not alone but *together*. Being a male, I am sure that when Adam first saw Eve coming to toward him his eyes strayed vertically from her neck down to her feet (I mean, c'mon, think about it; she was naked) before finally focusing on Eve's face—at which point he lovingly told her that she was now a part of him. He professed that they were connected as one. He whispered in her ear that they were part of each other now. "This is now bone of my bones and flesh of my flesh" (Genesis 2:23).

God himself officiated the first wedding. Adam spoke the first wedding vows and declared over Eve that they were connected together in the most intimate possible way. She was a part of him—body, soul, and spirit. They were two people united, two people becoming one. Togetherness.

So began their marriage journey in a beautiful garden under the skies that God had just created. Adam and Eve made love for the first time as husband and wife (have you ever wondered how long it took them to figure that part out? I mean, think about it—or not). They bore children and started the first family.

Everyone was healthy, and everyone was happy—until that day. That fateful day when Adam and Eve broke their relationship with God by sinning against him. At that moment, they opened the door for their marriage and family to become broken. God's judgment came. Togetherness was now going to be harder to keep. The door opened for anger, hostility, adultery, broken trust, and so many other togetherness destroyers to enter into their marriage. We know how from that day forward sin has destroyed marriages and torn apart families. It is still a reality in today's world. Unfortunately, that door is still open but for the grace of God. Through accepting Christ into our lives and receiving his forgiveness, his grace, and his salvation, we can do better through him. As we yield our hearts to the Holy Spirit, we can change and become people who can be happily married, be good parents, and continue to fulfill the same plan that God gave Adam and Eve. God's plan for men and women who meet someone they want to share togetherness with consists of them getting married, having kids, and dominating the world with their love for God. God still desires today what he did during the Garden of Eden days. He desires men and women to come together in marriage—to become one in body, soul, and spirit. To produce and raise children who will grow up to keep the human race going until Jesus comes back. God is pro-marriage. God is pro-children. God is pro-you.

Togetherness Is God's Strategy

"Then God said, 'Let us make mankind in our image, in our likeness, so that they may rule over the fish in the sea and the birds in the sky, over the livestock and all the wild animals, and over all the creatures that move along the ground'" (Genesis 1:26 NIV).

Multiplying takes togetherness. Governing and ruling the earth takes togetherness. Reigning over creation takes togetherness.

Husbands and wives were meant to rule the earth together, with each spouse fulfilling a calling and as a couple establishing God's kingdom on earth. Satan understands this strategy, and his first attack recorded in Scripture was on Adam and Eve's togetherness.

Satan is the father of lies, and he distorts the truth. He used this tactic when he made contact with Eve and played to her desire to be like God. Eve gave into that desire and Satan's temptation. She ate the fruit in front of her husband, fully aware of what she was doing. Adam stood by passively, watching Eve disobey the Lord. Adam didn't try to protect her by stopping her. Nor did he himself refrain from taking a bite. He also didn't try to defend her or cover her actions before God when he came calling.[1]

Together they sinned. Together they were judged. Together they lived the rest of their lives under the burden of the curses placed on them by God. Eve was no longer the perfect wife and was now put under subjection to Adam's sinful domination. She suffered because of it. Women have suffered sinful men's domination ever since.

Adam was no longer the perfect husband. He was relegated to living in a barren land, working by the sweat of his brow and scratching out a living for his family. He was now at odds with his wife, and their relationship suffered. They saw their two sons, Cain and Abel, no longer experiencing sibling togetherness, and their relationship ending when Cain murdered Abel. Togetherness was gone. God wants it restored.

Chapter 2

Cultural View of Marriage

In order for togetherness to be restored, we have to go back to what the Bible says about the original purpose of marriage. God designed marriage to be one man and one woman for life. But human culture changes, and we have drifted away from what God intended marriage to be. The biggest recent development on the culture front happened on June 26, 2015. That was the day the United States Supreme Court ruled in a five-to-four decision that state bans on same-sex marriages were no longer legal. In other words, all states must recognize and allow to be performed marriages of same-sex people. This ruling has opened the door for same-sex marriage in every state, no matter how the voting citizens in those states that had same-sex marriage bans feel about it. Their laws were overruled. Is it time to panic? No. God is still on his throne. His word is still true. His way will shine through the darkness. Let's face it, culture is going to continually drift away from Biblical directives on how to live life according to God's will. Even so, the United States Supreme Court certainly has no authority to change what God has already defined. This is a cultural change, not a Biblical change. And more cultural changes are coming. Not to depress you, but same-sex marriage is just the beginning. Now that this door has been opened, society won't stop at same-sex marriage. Society will feel responsible to eventually allow "whosoever will" to get married. It's important for Christ's followers to remember that we now live in a post-Christian nation. God is no longer honored nor respected in the town square or in our court justice system. He has been removed from every area of our nation except our houses of worship. Thank God we still live in a nation that does allow for freedom of worship. But we can't expect the Biblical worldview to coincide with the cultural worldview of marriage or sexuality. Those days have passed. Churches must be strong, stay the course, and teach the truth.

I'd like to look at three current cultural views of marriage, and then we'll go back to God's original view of marriage.

View # 1: Marriage is optional.

Today couples ask each other the question, "Why get married?"

A couple is young, childless, and free. Why get married?

A couple wants to test the relationship first before committing. Why get married?

A couple regularly engages in sex even though they aren't married. Why get married?

A couple has kids together, and the shared parenting arrangement seems to be working out. Why get married?

A single mom loves her boyfriend, who keeps asking her to marry him, but she hated her stepdad, and just thinking about bringing one into her home upsets her. Why get married?

Modern-day research reports that 50 percent of married couples have lived together before marriage. In the 1960s that percentage was 8 percent. Cohabitation has become the new normal. In the United States, the National Center for Health

Statistics issued a report recently showing that more and more people are living together and having kids before marriage. The report showed that the average duration of the first cohabitation was twenty-two months. *USA Today* reported that 48 percent of unmarried women aged fifteen to forty-four have cohabited before marriage, with 19 percent having children within the first year of living with someone.[1]

According to a *Wall Street Journal* article from March 2013, "Twenty-somethings are driving America's all-time high level of nonmarital childbearing, which is now at 41 percent of all births, according to vital-statistics data from the Centers for Disease Control and Prevention. Sixty percent of those births are to women in their early twenties, while teens account for only one-fifth of nonmarital births. Between 1990 and 2008, the teen pregnancy rate has dropped by 42 percent, while the rate of nonmarital childbearing among twenty-something women has risen by 27 percent."[2] Amazingly enough, those hurt the most by cohabitation are women and children. Yet women seem more than willing to avoid marriage—to their own detriment. Studies show the negative impact that single motherhood has on society. Those who are burdened with this life usually live close to the poverty line. Welfare, food stamps, and government assistance become their long-term sustenance instead of short-term help during a time of crisis. Fatherless children have higher rates of crime and substance use than do children of married parents. But society ignores this and chooses cohabitation and premarital sex anyway. Andrew Cherlin, in his book *The Marriage-Go-Round*, made an observation regarding the cohabitation trend. According to Cherlin, cohabitation is not just about financial expediency or wanting to live together just to try each other out. He writes about a bigger psychological paradigm shift that occurred after the 1950's. "The great growth of cohabiting relationships and the doubling of the divorce rate since then can't be tied to an increase in restlessness because there wasn't one. *Rather, these trends reflect the spread of an individualistic view of family life that emphasizes personal growth*[3] (emphasis mine). God designed marriage as a "giving" proposition. Society views marriage as a "getting" proposition. Men and women are to give of themselves to their spouses through serving one another, encouraging each other, and being there for the other when there is need. But now marriage and relationships have shifted to a "me" emphasis. "What's in this relationship for me? What benefit is there for me? What responsibilities can I avoid having to fulfill by not committing to marriage?" God designed togetherness as an "us" focused relationship instead of a "me" focused relationship. Women willing to cohabitate want a man. Men willing to cohabitate want a woman. And they both want sex *without the commitment* that Biblical marriage requires. The Bible calls this sin. Culture calls this convenience. In 2002, the National Marriage Project released a study entitled "Why Men Won't Commit," by Barbara Defoe Whitehead and David Popenoe. Pastor and author Timothy Keller shares a quote from this study in his book, *The Meaning of Marriage: Facing The Complexities Of Commitment*, that accurately describes why men gravitate towards living together rather than marriage. "Cohabitation gives men regular access to the domestic and sexual ministrations of a girlfriend while allowing them to lead a more independent life and continue to look around for a better partner."[4] Ouch. The truth hurts. Sex without the commitment to marriage and to marital fidelity is like a TV show with the viewer holding a remote control. The viewer is thinking, "I'll enjoy the 'show,' but when I'm bored with it or a better show comes on, I'll change the channel." Cohabitation is an easy way in and provides an even easier way out. You can just leave without the hassle and cost of divorce. Easy-squeezy.

In talking to couples who live together, most of whom profess to follow Jesus, the most common rationalization I hear is, "Well, we live together because it's easier financially than living alone." Other reasons people live together are having bad examples of marriage from their own parents, fear of making a long-term commitment to one person, financial instability, independence, and pride. None of these reasons justify living together according God's Word. Marriage is not optional when a man and a woman want to live under the same roof and share the same bed.

View #2: Marriage is disposable.

Let me say that that divorce is a serious subject. There are many other books and resources available that will give a much more in-depth look at it than I will here.

Togetherness is designed to strengthen marriages for couples who are willing to work at staying together. But I do want to take a brief moment to share with you what I've found to be the start of marriages crumbling and eventually dissolving. My goal here is to make you aware, so that you can be sensitive to it and stop it before it's too late, if that's possible.

Divorce is accepted as a common and viable option in today's culture. In 1969 my home state of California became the first state to allow couples to obtain divorce by simply telling the court that their marriage was broken and they wanted to end it, even without spousal agreement. This is known as a *no-fault* divorce. Another common term used is *irreconcilable differences.* This means that no one spouse will have to be blamed for the marriage not working out. Before no-fault divorce existed, simply saying that the marriage was beyond repair was not enough for a court to grant a divorce. Before 1969, divorce courts would make the couple prove that there was abuse, desertion, or adultery before granting divorce. By 1989, a mere twenty years after no-fault divorce was created, divorce rates shot up as high as 50 percent of all marriages. Making divorce easier resulted in an increase of the volume of marriages dissolving and more acceptance as a viable option for marriages in trouble.

In some happier news, the tide does seem to be turning. The Census Bureau reported in May of 2013 that "long-lasting marriages" are on the rise. Also, please forget the myth of the "50 percent *Christian* couple divorce rate." Ed Stetzer, a respected Christian researcher, reported that "couples who regularly practice any combination of serious religious behaviors and attitudes; attend church nearly every week; read their Bibles and spiritual materials regularly; pray privately and together; do enjoy significantly lower divorce rates then general public or unbelievers."[5] It would appear that a couple's taking their faith seriously plays an important role in keeping them together.

What about marriages that are ending and seem beyond repair?

Scripturally, there are valid reasons for a couple to dissolve their marriage. Adultery and abandonment are among them. Physical, verbal, and mental abuse can also justify divorce in extreme cases. The point I'm going to make here is that all the reasons why couples split up (valid or invalid) have the same root cause: hardness of heart. Jesus teaches us this, when he was asked by the religious leaders of the day whether divorce for any cause is lawful.

> Some Pharisees came to him to test him. They asked, "Is it lawful for a man to divorce his wife for any and every reason?" "Haven't you read," he replied, "that at the beginning the Creator 'made them male and

female,' and said, 'For this reason a man will leave his father and mother and be united to his wife, and the two will become one flesh'? So they are no longer two, but one flesh. Therefore, what God has joined together, let no one separate."

"Why then," they asked, "did Moses command that a man give his wife a certificate of divorce and send her away?"

Jesus replied, "Moses permitted you to divorce your wives because *your hearts were hard* (emphasis mine). But it was not this way from the beginning. I tell you that anyone who divorces his wife, except for sexual immorality, and marries another woman, commits adultery." (Matthew 19:3–9 NIV)

The root reason people divorce each other is they allow their hearts to harden toward their spouses. The word *hardness* is from the Greek word *sklerokardria*. *Skleros*, or hardness, is where we get the English word "sclerosis," and *kardian* is where the English word "cardiac" comes from. It describes a hardening of the heart.

Sclerosis is an abnormal hardening of body tissue. The most commonly known sclerosis is multiple sclerosis, which damages a person's nerve cells in the brain and spinal cord. Symptoms can include numbness, speech impairment, decreased muscular coordination, blurred vision, and slurred speech. This is a horrible condition of the human body that affects many people, including friends of mine. Sclerosis is a hardening of a person's body that causes it to shut down and not function as it is supposed to.

Hardness of the heart in regard to marriage has a similar effect on the relationship between a husband and wife. Communication begins to shut down. Feelings of love begin to turn into feelings of bitterness and resentment. Anger begins to expose itself in the form of verbal abuse and physical endangerment. Sexual intimacy occurs less frequently or ceases altogether. As a result, husbands or wives become more vulnerable to the temptation of adultery. A "hardening" has set in and begins its destructive work, ultimately killing a marriage.

The key to maintaining a "soft" heart in marriage begins with a personal relationship with Jesus. This may sound strange at first, but it's a powerful truth. You should love Jesus more than your spouse. Loving Jesus more than your husband or wife will result in the ability to love your husband or wife the way they need to be loved. Jesus fills our hearts with his love, which keeps our hearts soft and enables us to love our spouses more. It's a supernatural love.

The more time I spend with Jesus in his word, praying and worshiping, the more I love his people. Often I meet "unlovable" people, those who are hard to love. As a pastor I am called to love them anyway. I cannot do this without God's supernatural love pouring into me daily, filling me up and spilling out onto others. I pray every day that God will give me his love for others so that I can love that way too! (I also pray that God will help me to be easy for others to love as well—it goes both ways.)

The same principle applies to my wife, Autumn. She is very easy to love. She is beautiful, positive, fun, and easygoing. But she isn't perfect, and there are times when she is a little harder to love (I will leave it at that) and vice versa. As hard as it is to believe, I am not the perfect husband. It is during those times of "hardening" that I need God's love to overflow in my heart and spill over to her. And, like me, she also needs God's love to overflow in her heart and spill over to me. It is God's love that gives us the ability to overcome impatience, anger, and harsh words. When I fail in this, I can usually trace it back to a lack of prayer. My flesh, my humanness, and my weaknesses are expressed toward those I love the most. It seems to be easier to hurt them when I am not right with God and filled with his supernatural love.

Loving Jesus also results in us being emotionally healthy and whole. When I counsel singles who are preparing for marriage, I include this principle: "Find someone who loves Jesus more than you." People who love Jesus more than another person will look to him to make them whole and fill the needs in their lives. They will look to their spouses for companionship, fun, and adventure. They will want to create families and share ministry. The odds of developing a "hard heart" toward their spouses will be less if they love Jesus first and their spouses second.

Don't be jealous of Jesus! Be happy if you are number two to his number one. It is God's perfect design for your marriage.

I often ask couples what life would be like if each spouse treated the other in a Galatians 5:22 kind of way: "But the fruit of the Spirit is love, joy, peace, patience, kindness, goodness, faithfulness, gentleness, self-control." Can you imagine?—a marriage full of unconditional love, a fun atmosphere of joy and laughter, with patience for us when we are running late, kindness instead of meanness, goodness instead of bad treatment, faithfulness in sexuality, gentleness in communication and affection, self-control in the financial and emotional arena? Wow! It's wishful thinking, but I would like to think that married couples could live this life. It takes both husband and wife to love Jesus more than each other and to spend time with him, allowing him to change their hearts and fill them with love. It takes the Holy Spirit's adding God's "super" to our human love and emotions. I say, give it a try! You have nothing to lose and everything to gain.

Marriage is not disposable in God's eyes. There are ways to make it work and last a lifetime. I understand that in some cases divorce is acceptable and even necessary for the sake of those involved. Each case is individual and needs to be worked out with a pastor, counselor, and each other. Sometimes it just doesn't work and can't be saved, and that is where God's grace steps in and helps you get through it and get on with life. The main point of this section is to point out the fact that our society enters marriage with divorce seen as an easy option to exit for any reason. That is not the way God sees divorce. "'For I hate divorce!' says the Lord, the God of Israel" (Malachi 2:16).

View #3: Marriage is traditional.

God, in Scripture, defined marriage as "between one man and one woman for life," and this was universally accepted culturally for generations. At present, that definition is seen as "traditional" in the negative sense, meaning old-fashioned. Society's definition and the rules of marriage have changed. And it's a bit shocking to see where it has led us.

"Marriage is old-school from back in the day."

"Marriage is what Mom and Dad did, and it didn't work out for them."

"Marriage is worth avoiding at all costs."

"Marriage is a hassle."

"Marriage is expensive."

"Marriage is a commitment I'm not willing to make."

Marriage has a price that all are not willing to pay in this day and age of independence and entitlement.

Untraditional Marriage

Apparently there are new terms describing the current untraditional views of marriage. Ryan T. Anderson, in an article he wrote for the

Heritage Foundation entitled, "The Social Costs of Abandoning the Meaning of Marriage,"[6] described the latest terms that have been coined to describe this new outlook on marriage.

Monogamish is a situation wherein a partner would allow sexual infidelity, provided the spouse was honest about it. Can you imagine? "Honey, I'm home. How was your day? Mine was great. Had some very productive meetings at the office. Oh yeah, speaking of productive meetings, I hooked up with the VP of Sales during lunch break. She came on to me, and I couldn't help myself. Just thought you should know. What's for dinner?"

Polyamory describes a person who is "in love" or romantically involved with more than one person simultaneously. In other words, a man can be married to a woman he loves and have a girlfriend that he loves at the same time. But in polyamory, all parties involved are in agreement with this relational arrangement and willing to participate.

Throuple is a word created to be similar to *couple* but mean involving three people. Throuple is more involved then polymory, in that throuples have a permanent domestic living arrangement. For example, two women and a man living together would share all aspects of life as if they were married to each other.

Wedlease is a term that defines marriage as a short-term commitment with an "out clause" at the end of the wedlease term of their choosing. Instead of a couple making a lifelong commitment to each other, as at a traditional wedding ceremony, they make a three-year, five-year, or ten-year commitment period. When the lease time is up, they can decide to walk away without the hassle of divorce proceedings, or they can decide to renew the wedlease for another term. Apparently, marriage is now on equal footing with leasing a car!

The reason things fall under the category of "traditional" is that they work! That's why they are now traditions, being passed on from generation to generation. My family has a Christmas tradition of baking a special bread that is a secret recipe passed down from generation to generation from my Dad's side of the family. My oldest daughter has now been brought into the family secret so she can bake the bread for her family. It's a small thing, but it's meaningful. It makes us closer as a family. Its tradition.

For thousands of years, traditional marriage between one man and one woman has served the world well. God's design for marriage has been faithfully carried out, producing happy and fulfilled people as well as producing children to propagate the human race, just as God commanded Adam and Eve to do in the beginning. It's a good system. Whenever we try to improve on what God designed, we fall well short and make life miserable for ourselves. God designed it right the first time. Let's stick to the plan! The next chapter discusses how God looks at marriage.

Chapter 3

God's View of Marriage

First, God's view of marriage is that of a *covenant* versus society's view of marriage as a *contract*. Those two words paint a clear picture of the difference between God's view of marriage and society's view. Covenant and contract.

In *a contract*-based marriage (disclaimer: by contract I'm not referring to an actual contract signed by both parties; it's more of a mind-set entering into the marriage) the vows are a bilateral agreement between the husband and wife, dependent upon the performance of the agreement. If one of the spouses fails to uphold his/her end of the agreement, then the other spouse has no obligation to perform his/her end and is no longer bound by the terms of the vows and can end the marriage. In a contract-based marriage, the couples wait and see if things work out. They wait to see if their spouses perform to the expectations set by the vows. If not, they quit the marriage, file for divorce, haggle with the attorneys, fight for child custody, and then find someone who (they hope) can perform better in the next marriage.

In a *covenant*-based marriage, the vows are a God-initiated, unalterable, unchangeable, irreversible commitment until "death do us part." Marriage under covenant is a sacred bond between a husband and wife and between the couple and God.

In a covenant-based marriage the wedding ceremony has strong spiritual meaning and is seen as holy before God.

Even though marriage includes an element of civil law under each state government, under covenant terms marriage is instituted under divine law, and couples are accountable for their marriage to God and his Word as well as to the people who witnessed the wedding. Covenant is commitment based and doesn't depend upon the performance of either party. It's a covenant of love for love's sake. It's love covering the sins and weaknesses of our spouses. It's love that stays married through the tough times, love that is willing to work difficult things out. It's husband and wife committed to staying together, to being faithful to each other until the day when one of them goes to heaven without the other.

As I write this, my parents have been married for sixty years. They are a true example of covenant marriage, even though it didn't start out that way. When I was a young boy, I would wake up to yelling, screaming, and occasionally the sound of things being thrown. When I turned twelve, divorce court was where my Mom was planning to go. She'd had enough. Before following through with filing divorce papers, she was invited to attend a Christian women's retreat by a friend of hers. My mom decided to attend, and her life was changed forever. She met Jesus that weekend and made him her Savior. She came back different. Her new Christian friends counseled her to pray for my dad and give him another chance. They encouraged her to see that divorce wasn't God's best and that my dad could change, with her newfound faith now in play. She heeded their advice and stuck with my dad. He wasn't easy to live with back then. But he noticed such a change in my mom that he became interested in learning about Jesus for himself. Three months after mom became a follower of Christ, my dad made the same decision. He began the journey of following Jesus and became a new man. It took a while to get some stuff healed up and out of his life, but his heart toward my mom softened and vice versa. They sought help and did the work needed to each become a better spouse. They made it through the storm. They kept their marriage covenant intact. I'm glad to say that they are happier now than ever. It's actually embarrassing to be with them in public, they are so in love and affectionate. I'm now in my fifties and still saying things like, "Mom and Dad, that's gross, please don't do that in public." They made a commitment to honor the covenant they made before God to each other (even though they didn't know God personally at the time of their marriage) and to work out the tough bits. They determined to find healing for their hurts and to change their attitudes, behaviors, and conversations toward each other. Covenant won.

It's important to know that even though the traditional marriage vows use covenantal language, if the mind-set is of a contract-based marriage, then that marriage is likely to fail when things get tough.

Andreas J. Köstenberger, in his book *God, Marriage, and Family: Rebuilding the Biblical Foundation*, gives "5 marriage covenant implications."[1] According to Köstenberger, covenantal marriage is seen as *permanent;*[2] *sacred*, that is, precious and holy to God,[3] *intimate*, with a man and woman "leaving" their parents and "cleaving" to each other;[4] *beneficial*, with both husband and wife caring for each other;[5] and *exclusive*, with no other person coming between them.[6] I encourage you to take a moment and read the Bible verses listed after each implication, found at the back of the book. It will deepen the meaning of the marriage vows you may have spoken years ago.

Covenant marriage is based on a *covenant* love. Covenant love is based on *commitment*.

Societal marriage is based on a *contract* love. Contract love is based on *performance*.

Second, God's view of marriage is as a heterosexual joining of two people in a partnership. Despite what governments feel is right and society dictates as true, the Bible is clear. Genesis 2:24 leaves no question as to who God designed marriage for: "This explains why a man leaves his father and mother and is joined to his wife, and the two are united into one." In their book, *Same-Sex Marriage: A Thoughtful Approach to God's Design for Marriage*, authors Sean McDowell and John Stonestreet describe well God's purpose for heterosexual marriage. "Man and woman coming together in the marital union, the most intimate, secure, long-lasting and consequential way that two can come together, really creates a full, human whole—it brings together into a cooperative relationship the two distinct and necessary parts of humanity. This is no small thing."[7] Men and women were purposefully created different by God to complement each other. Equals in value, different in nature, they are designed to work together to create families and honor God.

For those who hold the Bible as the authoritative Word of God regarding all things for this life, there is no alternative interpretation.

Third, God's view of marriage is that the marriage covenant is not to be broken. Husbands and wives are instructed to "be united" to each other.[8] *United* means to be joined together, to cleave to, cling to, hold on tightly and never let go. As I mentioned earlier, divorce should not be considered as an option unless circumstances are such that pastors and Christian counselors both agree that the couple should be released from their marriage because things are so bad or dangerous. These circumstances are very rare, but they do exist. For every couple who hold Christ in the center of their personal lives and their marriage, divorce shouldn't ever even be mentioned. That's what a covenant is—commitment to stay together until death. This breeds security and enables couples to really talk things out honestly, because they know that whatever the circumstances or challenges they are facing they will work it out and stay together. When divorce is a threat that hangs over the marriage, then spouses hide things in their hearts out of fear that the other will leave them if they discuss them or confront the issue head-on. The threat of divorce is an evil weapon we use on each other. Listen everybody: you are married. It's God's will that you stay that way! Stay true to your marriage vows. Don't break the covenant. I've heard it said that you can't "un-one something that's been one-d." Bad grammar for sure, but it makes the point.

Fourth, God's view of marriage is a man and woman becoming as one person. Genesis 2:24 goes on to say that the man, Adam, "is united to his wife, and they become one flesh." Husband and wife become united in body (sexual expression). They become united in soul (mind, will, and emotional connection) and united in spirit (spiritual unity). Autumn and I have been married for thirty-two years, and we've experienced the becoming-one phenomenon. Our sex life is better than ever ('nuff said). We've connected emotionally at a deep level, where we each know what the other is thinking. We know what the other would do in just about every circumstance, and we feel what the other feels (empathy) even though we are polar opposites in just about every way. We have become one without sacrificing our unique personalities or our likes and dislikes. Spiritually, we share our expressions of faith and service in our local church. We came from different theological backgrounds on many different levels. Together, as a young couple, we studied the Bible and listened to teaching from our spiritual leaders. We grew in spiritual unity as we prayed together and discussed what we were learning. We were able to share common beliefs *together*, and now *together* we share those with others. I honestly think that the two-are-united-in-one dynamic can't be totally understood until a couple has been married for twenty-five years. It is truly amazing and makes the latter half of married life the absolute best!

Fifth, God's view of marriage is human companionship, intimacy, and baby-making. Togetherness in marriage is a beautiful thing consisting of three parts: companionship, intimacy, and procreation.

Togetherness is Companionship

Marriage is usually the end result of a friendship gone good. A man and woman meet and become friends. A *friend* has been defined as "a person whom one knows and with whom one has a bond of mutual affection, typically exclusive of sexual or family relations." In other words, a guy and gal like being together. Then, as time goes on, they really like being together. Then they discover that they really, really, really like being together. Then they decide that they want to have sex together. (Men really, really, really, really, really want to have sex. *Oops!* As I wrote that, Autumn reminded me that women really want to have sex too. My bad!) They decide to marry each other so that they can be together always and forever. Sturdy homes are constructed on a strong concrete foundation. The strong foundation of marriage is friendship. A husband and wife should enjoy each other and share interests, experiences, adventures, simple pleasures, laughter, and responsibilities. When storms of life hit and the *marriage* isn't working so well, the *friendship* should still be intact. It's friendship that saves marriages. Friends *work together* to *stay together*. When Autumn and I face difficulties in our marriage, we always bring it back to the fact that we are friends. We aren't going to let anything stand in the way of or break apart our friendship. It's our friendship that gives us the ability, the desire, and the time to work things out.

God saw that it wasn't good for man to be alone.[9] Mankind was not created to live life in isolation. Outside of a personal relationship with God, companionship is the most basic need a human being has. Babies need parents to care for them in order to survive. Children need other children to play with in order to have healthy self-images. Adults need people to share meaningful experiences with. Research has shown that solitary confinement in prisons has extremely negative effects. In an interview with *Wired.com*, Craig Haney, a psychologist at the University of California, Santa Cruz, who is an expert on the effects of long-term solitary confinement, says that people in solitary confinement suffer from "isolation panic." They have difficulty being alone. This can cause them "to lose their grasp of their identity." Isolation "undermines one's sense of self." Their emotions are stunted, because there is no one giving them feedback on how they are feeling. Without the feedback of others, it becomes a "struggle to maintain sanity." People in isolation can also be "easily manipulated." Some lose the "ability to control themselves" in regard to anger, or they become deeply depressed. It's obvious that God meant for us to experience togetherness. Sharing togetherness with someone who loves us provides balance, joy, fulfillment, and emotional well-being.[10]

God's intention was that there would be no greater companion than the person you are married to. God brings us together so we can survive and thrive. That means being friends first.

Togetherness Is Intimacy

Intimacy means peeling back the layers and allowing someone to see the total you. It's connecting with a person beyond shallow conversation. Intimacy involves sharing feelings, emotions, fears, needs, disappointments, and frustrations. There are three levels of intimacy that togetherness brings.

The first level is *emotional intimacy*. Emotional intimacy involves our feelings. This level of intimacy takes place when undivided attention is given while communication is taking place. Emotional intimacy takes place when honesty, understanding, and acceptance of how our spouse feels happens in our conversation. Emotional intimacy takes place when feelings are shared and validated by the other person. Emotional intimacy takes place when understanding and sensitivity are shown. Emotional intimacy takes place when forgiveness is asked for and received. Emotional intimacy takes place when there is safety in sharing needs. Emotional intimacy takes place when sadness, grief, fear, and disappointment are expressed without fear of rejection or ridicule. Emotional intimacy takes place during dates and shared activities. It means letting go and letting in—letting go of what's inside the heart by talking and sharing with each other, and letting the other person in by allowing sharing of thoughts, feelings, and dreams.

The second level of intimacy is *spiritual intimacy*. This level of intimacy is the most neglected and the hardest to connect between spouses. But once the connection is made, it's an impossible bond to break. Spiritual intimacy happens by praying together and talking about insights into the Bible together. Spiritual intimacy happens by attending a local church together and getting involved in a small group of spiritually minded people. Spiritual intimacy happens by worshiping together and serving in ministry together.

The third level of intimacy is *sexual intimacy*. Sexual intimacy is being comfortable in the bedroom together. Sexual intimacy is being satisfied with a spouse's response to sexual needs and desires. Sexual intimacy is when there is mutual initiation by both partners. Sexual intimacy is the ability to talk about sexual preferences, sharing likes and dislikes, without embarrassment or intimidation. Sexual intimacy is a sense of adventure in trying something new and fun. We'll discuss this more in Part Five: Sleeping Together.

Togetherness Is Procreation

Togetherness in marriage is the foundation for the "be fruitful and increase in number" part of life that was commanded by God.[11] Children are a blessing from God. "Children are a gift from the Lord; they are a reward from him" (Psalm 127:3 NLT). God's desire for the human race is that we increase through procreation. He loves children, and to get them he tricked us. He made babies super cute, so we'll want to have them. He made the baby-making process super fun so that we'll want to make them. Way to go, God—thank you for both! Children are highly valued in God's eyes. He has a plan for us, our kids, and our families. We'll discuss children and parenting in more detail in Part Six: Parenting Together.

Setting Realistic Expectations

Coming together is not easy. It's beautiful and messy at the same time. Two individuals who come together don't necessarily fit together in every area of life. When we put a puzzle together, the pieces fit perfectly, resulting in a picture that everyone recognizes. A complete puzzle has no missing pieces or gaps. (Ask me how I know about puzzles with missing pieces. I'm an expert.)

The marriage puzzle is the opposite. Two lives come together, but there are pieces missing. There are gaps, because two individual lives don't interconnect perfectly. This is where love, grace, forgiveness, and selflessness come in. It is in our imperfections that the beauty of togetherness is seen. Two imperfect people do their best to fill in the missing pieces and bridge the gaps in order to make a marriage. Trouble arises when people come together in marriage with expectations that can't be met. In the movie *Jerry Maguire*, the Tom Cruise line, "You complete me," is completely false, though it made for a very touching romantic moment (or an eye-roll moment, depending on which gender you are). There is no person on earth who can complete another. Only God can bring wholeness to our lives. Some people live with a fantasy or illusion that if they marry the person of their dreams their hurts will be healed, and they will finally become whole, because their spouses are the missing pieces in the puzzle of life. They naively think that any gaps they have in their lives will be filled by their spouses. The danger here is that eyes that should be looking to God for healing and wholeness are looking at human beings, who will never be able to give what only God can provide. The spouses are now in the position of God and being looked upon to bring wholeness. That will fail. Heartbreak and disappointment will come, and togetherness will be strained. I hope this book will help to fill some gaps and give you some tools to help you work *together* and experience what we all want more of—*togetherness*.

Part Two

Talking Together

Chapter 4

Meaningful Conversation

Autumn and I struggled in this area in the first years of our marriage. She came from a talkative family, where everyone shared experiences, feelings, opinions, and emotions. When her family gathered together, it was loud. Everybody knew everybody's business, and they all had opinions they were willing to share. My family talked, but we were more reserved. My family consisted of a sister, my parents, and me. We were pretty low-key as far as volume went.

Personally, I'm private and protective. I find it hard to share how I'm feeling about something. I'm quick to share opinions but not feelings. So I hold things in and let things go, or I deal with things internally. That's not healthy, I know. I'm trying to get better at letting others in. I also am quick to think of a solution to a problem; I'm a fixer. That's not always a good thing as far as Autumn is concerned.

Autumn finds help in talking things through, sometimes over and over and over again. I just need to say something once and move on. She even talks to herself as she is working through something. I don't mean that in a funny or weird way. It seriously helps her to process and find answers. She is an auditory person who processes by hearing solutions out loud. She is also a deeply feeling-oriented person. Her emotions get involved in every aspect of her life. I love her for that. Me, I'm not so much a feeling person. I am practical and logical in my thought process. When I am processing things through, it appears that I shut down because I don't talk much. I'm also a visual person who sees solutions as pictures in my imagination. So I don't always connect with Autumn when she's feeling something. She doesn't always connect with me when I'm not talking. This causes disconnects when we talk together. Our differences came to a head one day about twelve years into our marriage.

I was working in my home office, and Autumn asked if she could come in and talk with me. I invited her in, and she began to share a frustration that she was experiencing. She *felt* deeply about it. She was angry, stressed, and needing to work this out. In my matter-of-fact manner, I suggested what I thought she should do. I *didn't* feel deeply about it. In fact, I didn't feel anything at all. I just went straight to the solution. "This is an easy fix," I said, and I told her what she should do. I provided a solution, with the attitude, *Now do it and move on.* End of conversation.

My response made her angry. She doesn't usually get angry. But she was mad and very frustrated. "You don't understand, and you obviously don't care!" I was taken aback by that accusation. She stormed out of my office, which was so out of her character that I sat back in my chair, stunned at her reaction.

"What's her problem?" I muttered and went back to my laptop.

A few minutes later, she came back into my office. She calmly said, "You're not getting what I'm communicating to you, and it's frustrating to me. I told you how I *feel*, but I don't think you get it. So let me try again. I want to paint you a picture. Imagine you are a cat, and you are backed into a corner, surrounded by a pack of big, mean, barking dogs. Can you see that?"

I could visualize that scenario in my imagination. "Yes, I can see that," I replied.

"By the look of the cat, can you feel what that cat is feeling?" she asked.

"Sure. Afraid, trapped, insecure, like there is no way out," I said.

Autumn breathed a big sigh. "That is how I'm feeling right now because of this situation. I just need you to feel it with me, so you can help me." Wow. It was an *aha* moment for me, a true revelation of my lack of ability to communicate adequately with my wife. At that moment I felt as if we were communicating at a deeper level than ever before. I got it. She got it. For me to feel what she was feeling, she needed to paint a *visual* picture for me. From that picture, I could attach my feelings and at some level connect my feelings with her feelings. That's what she needed for us to be able to talk together. I learned that when I wanted her to see something that, as a visual person, I *saw*, I had to connect a *feeling* with it so that she could connect with me and see what I saw. It was a breakthrough moment for us.

Words Have Power

Words have hidden power behind them that can affect people emotionally, both for the positive and for the negative.

Words can build a person up or tear them down.

Words can change a negative environment into a positive environment.

Words can build up, encourage, and strengthen your spouse.

Words can tear down, discourage, and weaken your spouse.

Proverbs 18:21 says, "The tongue has the power of life and death." Words are the finished product of the assembly line of our thoughts. The very thoughts that begin in our minds attach themselves to our emotions and come out of our mouths. This means the thoughts we have about our spouses will come out in our words. Scary thought, isn't it? This usually happens during an emotional outburst of frustration or anger, in the form of meanness or cutting sarcasm. Jesus said, "For the mouth speaks what the heart is full of. A good man brings good things out of the good stored up in him, and an evil man brings evil things out of the evil stored up in him. But I tell you that everyone will have to give account on the Day of Judgment for every empty word they have spoken. For by your words you will be acquitted, and by your words you will be condemned" (Matthew 12:34–37 NIV)

I like to say that we are all "tongue-tied." Our tongues are tied to the quality of our marriage relationships. As we will see in this section of *Togetherness*, communication in marriage is a key to success. Having two different people living together as one family under the same roof can be difficult, so it's important that we learn to communicate well with our spouses. Marriages can be destroyed with words. I've met with countless couples in my office who were so mean to each other that I thought to myself, *I would want out of this marriage too, if Autumn and I talked to each other that way.*

Don't blow up your marriage over words and an inability to communicate at a mature level. It takes work and effort. It takes being mature grown-ups, facing the difficulties and being willing to humble yourself, to listen to understand and then to ultimately change.

Proverbs 18:22 (NLT) is a powerful verse that is written to husbands: "The man who finds a wife finds a treasure, and he receives favor from the Lord." How do *you* treat treasure? Husbands, do you treat your guns, cars, or camping gear with more care then your wife? Treasure is considered extremely valuable. Do you *extremely* value your wife? Treasure is guarded and protected. Are you guarding and protecting your wife from things that would harm her or damage her? Treasure is cherished. Do you cherish your wife? To cherish her is to adore her, to care for her. Is she your *treasure*?

Wives, here is a verse for you, Proverbs 31:23 (NIV): "Her husband is respected at the city gate, where he takes his seat among the elders of the land."

Wives, are you giving and showing your husband the proper respect he deserves? To respect him is to admire and appreciate his achievements. Do you put him down to your friends? Do you embarrass him in public in the way you speak about him or treat him? Do you henpeck him or treat him like a little boy? Are you acting like his mom instead of his wife? Do you *respect* him with your words and actions?

In a nutshell, every word counts! Talking together is what will keep you together, because your words are what you share together. Words are the glue to your relationship. Meaningful conversation brings life. Let's look at how this can happen for you.

Chapter 5

Connected Conversation

I bought a lamp for my office and was looking forward to having the extra lighting around my desk. I plugged the lamp in and— wait for it—nothing happened. No light. Not even a flicker. *Hmmm.* Must be a faulty connection. I unplugged the lamp from the top socket of the wall plug and plugged it into the bottom socket. The light bulb instantly turned on, and just like Day One of Creation, there was light. What had happened the first time? The top socket of the wall plug had a faulty connection, and thus there was no electricity to power the light bulb. When husbands and wives talk together, there must be a *meaningful connection* between them. The *current* of conversation must flow through both participants in order to power the conversation and make it *electric.* Let's look at how meaningful connections are made when people talk together.

Connection in conversation is made when we honor our spouses.

People respond to honor. There is something in all of us that appreciates being honored by others. It's natural and it's okay. It's being a normal human. If you want to make a deep connection in conversion, showing honor is a good place to begin.

Honor is a word that carries deep meaning when taken in context of its usage in the New Testament of the Bible. The word *honor* in the Greek language is *timao.* Its meaning is "to place value on." To honor your spouse is to place a value or worth on him or her. *Timao* is used sixteen times in the New Testament. All of those mentions in Scripture are in connection to human relationships, including those with family members, widows, and government leaders.[1] Two of the mentions refer to Jesus himself being valued, literally, at thirty pieces of silver.[2] Another mentions Jesus placing value on his relationship to his Father, God[3].

To honor your spouse when you are talking together is to place a high value on the conversation. This occurs when the feeling between you both is that there is no other place you'd rather be right there in that moment than with him or her. In effect you are saying, "Talking with you right now is my highest priority."

Honor is also placing a high value on the words and emotions expressed. Choosing words wisely, using discretion and discernment, is how you honor your words. Controlling your emotions when the conversation gets heated is how you honor your emotions in conversation. You show honor by not raising your voice or using insults to cut your spouse down to "put him in his place." Honor is not "scoring points" or "going for the win." It's showing love, kindness, and gentleness. Honor is understanding and trying to find the solution if one is needed, or at times, it's just listening to your spouse talk without saying much, because all she needs right then is to be heard.

The interesting thing about honor is that the value you place on your spouse is up to you. Honor is a free-market valuation. You can choose to place high value or low value on your spouse at that moment. The free-market principle of supply and demand doesn't determine the honor value. You do. The love in your heart makes that choice. This is difficult when behaviors and attitudes don't command high honor. I get that. At times immaturity, anger, laziness, and abuse lower the honor value. A lack of love for a wife and lack of respect for a husband lowers the honor value.

There have been times when I have said or done stupid things, and at those moments in time I wasn't worthy of much honor. But in most cases Autumn made a choice to honor me anyway. Instead of putting me down and telling me what a loser I was, she built me up and shared her concerns, which included pointing out my faults in those times. I felt honored, and that caused me to want to work it out, to change, to get better and correct my mistakes. When husbands and wives hammer each other and point fingers while pointing out faults, they dishonor themselves and their spouses. The results are never pretty. Relationship valuation is lowered, and negative results are experienced rather than helpful solutions. That's why it's important to come into a conversation, a talking-together moment, determined to show honor to your spouse. This is a decision that you make beforehand, not a result of how the conversation is going. The conversation will go well if honor is shown at the beginning and maintained all the way through until the time of talking together is over. Place a high honor value on the next upcoming chat, and see what a difference it makes.

Connection in conversation is made when we listen to each other.

Listening is an art. It's a skill. It's something that is learned over time through effort. Listening well, or being an active listener, as they say, is a powerful tool of connection. When a person speaks and shares his heart and feels listened to by the person on the other end of the conversation, he feels honored, validated and loved. But what is involved in being an active listener, more commonly known as a "good" listener? The goal of communication is mutual understanding. Talking is only half the equation. It's also the easiest part of the equation. Talking is easier then actively listening. Let me give you a few helpful hints on how to be a good active listener, with the goal of increasing mutual understanding.

First, and most commonly known, is eye contact. When you look your spouse in the eye, you are letting him know that there is nothing more important at this moment than listening to you. Eye contact keeps distractions at a minimum and allows you to focus on what is being communicated. Experts say that 60 percent of communication is body language, 30 percent of communication is the tone inflections of your voice (also known as "spirit of intent"), and only 10 percent of communication is the actual words you use. So, by making eye contact, you can tell more about what your spouse is communicating by seeing their facial expressions and body language than by the words they are speaking. Eye contact is key.

Second, leaning in toward your spouse lets her know you are engaged. Sitting forward with your face and hands closer to your spouse makes her feel you are interested in what she has to say more than if you are leaning back, slouched deep in the couch or slumped over with your arms crossed on a chair, looking bored. Leaning forward with elbows on a table, or sitting next to your spouse on the couch, holding hands, communicates that you are happy to listen and want to help.

Third, using verbal cues is another way to show interest and engagement. Try simple things like, "Wow," "That's amazing," "Oh man," "I'm sorry that happened," "That's awful," "I see," or "Tell me more about that." Little verbal responses make the one-way conversation a two-way conversation. Stone silence is awkward. But little verbal responses help keep the conversation fresh and the speaker more at ease to keep sharing.

Fourth, ask clarifying questions to bring more understanding. Oftentimes we don't really understand what has just been shared, so before we give a response, an idea, or opinion, we need to ask clarifying questions. "Can you tell me again exactly what was said when your boss called you into his office?" "What does that mean?" "Can you be more specific when describing what happened?" "Do you mean … when you say that?" "Did I hear you correctly in that …?" "So, what you are asking me is …?" As you learn the art of asking clarifying questions, you'll begin to understand more fully what your spouse is sharing. Asking questions is like peeling back the layers of an onion. Each question allows you to go deeper and get better results from your talk. I believe that it takes four clarifying questions to really get to the core of an issue with a person you are communicating with.

Lastly, I mentioned that the main component of communication is body language. You communicate more with your bodily positions and facial expressions than with your words. Your body should be facing your spouse, not turned away. Your arms should not be folded, as that signals disinterest, separation, and a defensive posture. Your face should have a smile—not a fake one but one that lets your spouse know you love and care for him. Your eyes should be looking directly into your spouse's eyes, communicating that you're present and in the moment. When your body shows you care, then words will carry greater meaning.

Connection in conversation is made when we know we are on the same team.

This one is a big one, and we'll address it more in depth in the chapter "Fighting Together," but let me introduce this powerful principle with you now, as it applies to making connections in conversation. Many people are very competitive. When they are going against another person, team, or player, they are playing for the victory. They are out to win and to make you lose. They are going to be on top, with you at the bottom, whatever it takes. This attitude is great for athletic competitions, board games, and business deals, but it makes for horrible conversation. When couples are talking together and it becomes a competition, mean things come out, emotions run hot, and usually one spouse wins and the other spouse loses, which really means both spouses lose. Connection in conversation comes about when both spouses remember they are on the *same team* and are not competitors. Playing on the same team brings camaraderie, a sense of working together, and companionship. This is key to overcoming disagreements and obstacles in marriage. Realize that you are in this together, and together you can talk this out and come to an agreement. Be on the same team.

There will be times when getting on the same team is difficult. But for resolution, unity, or a solution to a problem, you have to get yourselves back on the same team, working together to make your lives work.

Connection in conversation is made when all distractions are laid aside.

You can tell when a person you're communicating with isn't interested. Eyes are looking past you. The head is down. The phone is being checked. Texts are being sent as you speak. The television is being heard, and you're not. It's frustrating. You feel devalued, unimportant, and ignored. I remember, as a young man, being in a pastor's office and sharing my heart regarding something that I felt God was leading me into, and I needed some wise counsel. This was a huge life-changing decision for me. In the middle of my sharing my dreams, the pastor fell asleep. Literally. Eyes closed, heavy breathing, head nodding.

I kept talking, for some reason. I didn't know what else to do. Finally, his head snapped forward, and he woke himself up. He looked at me and smiled as if nothing had happened and said it sounded like a good idea and I should pursue it. I thanked him for his time, told him I was glad I could share his nap time with him and that he needed to wipe the drool off his shirt before his next appointment (I didn't say that—but I wanted to). Then I went and talked to someone else, who was more interested and actually stayed awake to hear my heart's dreams.

Connection in conversation happens when both spouses lay aside all distractions and focus solely on each other. Time and place are important for distractions to be limited. My wife knows that during a big sporting event on TV is not a good time to get my undivided attention for a serious conversation. I know that during her morning quiet time is not a good time to get her undivided attention for a serious conversation. Talking together means *talking* together—not talking/watching or talking/texting together. Talking together occurs when eye-to-eye and ear-to-ear conversation takes place. So be sure the TV is off, the kids are playing or in bed, phones are on silent, and you are in the mood for a meaningful chat. Distractions short-circuit conversation connections, resulting in a disconnected conversation that pulls couples apart instead of bringing them together.

Dr. Gary Chapman, author of the best-selling book, *The Five Love Languages*, describes meaningful conversation as "where two individuals are sharing their experiences, thoughts, feelings, and desires in a friendly, *uninterrupted* (emphasis mine) context."[4] Uninterrupted conversation takes coordination and planning. Couples must schedule alone time for the purpose of talking together. Here are some ideas for you.

Date Night: Plan times to go out and spend quality and quantity time together. However many dates a month you can squeeze in will help your communication. Going out for a meal is good, because you can talk to each other while looking at each other and enjoying a different atmosphere than at home.

Late Night: Couples with children in the home have the hardest time connecting in conversation. The kids need a lot of your time and attention. So for many, a couple's late night is the best time to talk together. When the kids are in bed and the house is quiet, you can talk together in a meaningful way. If you can stay up and remain alert, late-night conversations can be fun and meaningful—and if you say the right things, late-night conversation can lead to other late-night extracurricular activity (if you know what I mean). Talk about a "connection."

Coffee in the Morning: If you just can't stay awake late at night, then early morning coffee is a great time to talk. Morning people are wide-awake, energetic, and thinking clearly. This is a great option. If you connect for even twenty minutes in the morning, that conversation can carry you through the day. This might mean that one spouse needs to get up a little earlier than he or she would like in order to have the morning time before the other spouse heads off to work. But in the long run, it will be worth the schedule adjustment if it means better communication.

Shared Activity: Busy people sometimes only have one day off to unwind and connect. Talking together on a walk, a hike, or a bike ride can bring couples closer. Here is a hint for women who want to connect in conversation with their husbands: when you combine talking with doing a shared activity together with your husband, it is a win. He'll open up, have a bit of fun, and share more of himself with you. Autumn and I have had some of our best talks while on hiking trails or sitting on a sandy beach. Think ahead, make a plan, make it natural and organic, and you can have a great talking-together experience while having fun at the same time.

Connection in conversation is made when we focus on *common* needs.

In order for my desk lamp to operate properly, the lamp had to be plugged in, and electricity had to flow out so the bulb would light up. It takes two to light a lamp—the electricity and the bulb. The lamp of conversation operates on the same principle. A husband or wife starts the conversation, and the spouse responds with thoughts, ideas, and opinions. A wife asks a question, and the husband gives a thoughtful answer. A husband expresses an opinion, and the wife gives her opinion. It takes two to have a conversation. But for the conversation to become meaningful, it is necessary that each person focuses on the needs of the other just as much as on their own. Otherwise, talking together becomes "I'll talk and you listen." It becomes a one-sided it's-all-about-me conversation. No one likes to be spoken to without the ability to answer back or share thoughts and feelings. If we'll converse with each other with the goal of hearing *and* being heard, a lot of very good things will result.

Research has been done and books written about the differences between men and women, and for the most part, it's true. But there are common needs that husbands and wives share that can be met during times of talking together. Let's look at three of them.

Common Care: All human beings have a need to be cared for, a need for someone to love and be there for them. We need to have the security that comes from having people in our lives who will help during difficult times. There is a principle in the Bible regarding care. Peter is writing to church leaders, and as he is ending the letter, he gives them this exhortation: "Humble yourselves … casting all your care upon Him, for He cares for you."[5] The Greek word for care is *merimna,* which means "to divide the mind." A divided mind causes anxiety, discouragement, confusion, and fear about the future. Peter is telling church leaders to give God all of their care (anxiety, discouragement, confusion, and fear about the future) because God cares for them. The Greek word for cares is *melei*, which means "to care about, to think about, to make an appropriate response." So here is how this care-casting concept works. We give God our anxiety, and he gives us the appropriate response, which is that he loves us and will help us handle our cares through his grace, faithfulness, and miracle power. We "cast our care" by giving it to him in prayer. He gives us "His cares," responding to our need. This principle applies to married couples, in that when talking together we have a need to share our cares and then be cared for (given the appropriate response back). That could be a solution to a problem, an answer to a question, or a simple smile, hug, and verbal affirmation of support. When we talk together, we need to include care in the conversation.

Common Kindness: Nobody likes a meany. Whether it's the bully on the school playground or the mean boss who is unpleasant to be around, no one likes to talk to mean people. Kindness is essential to connection in talking together. Kindness brings security and creates a safe environment for sharing deep issues of the heart. It's kindness that joins people together and makes a difficult conversation easier for two people to engage in. Kindness is communicated with eye contact, smiles, and gentle voices. Humor and empathy are also powerful forms of kindness. Think back on your life for a minute. Who were your absolute favorite people? Most likely your favorite people were the kind ones. One of my favorite bosses was Dave, who managed the restaurant where I worked as a bus boy. I was a high school teenager, and Dave treated me kindly when I dropped and broke a case of expensive wine while stocking the wine cellar. *Crash!*

"O-o-o-ps. Sorry, Dave." Then there was the time I was carrying six drinks, including a couple of large glasses of milk for a couple of kids, and while I was lowering the tray to the table, I lost my balance and spilled the drinks all over the table and the laps of a family. He could have yelled, insulted me, and fired me. But he knew both these incidents were accidents, and though they were costly, he responded in kindness. I wanted to work hard for Dave after his act of kindness. And thirty-five years later, I still remember it.

Mean words cut deep. Brutal responses to someone's feelings and experiences harden hearts. Walls go up. Isolation sets in. Married couples drift apart. Lack of kindness kills conversation and can eventually kill a marriage.

Common Validation: In talking together, we need to master how to validate each other. To validate is to demonstrate support for what is being said and the person saying it. Notice I didn't say *agree* with what is being said. Disagreement is common, healthy, and valuable to a marriage. Having two differing opinions is helpful when solving problems or addressing serious issues. Validating simply says, "I might not agree you on this subject, but I support you as an individual to think this way. You are smart and capable, and I am going to work with you on this to come to agreement. I value you and your opinions." Many times, talking together turns into a verbal boxing match, as both spouses try to make their own point and discredit the other's viewpoint by making fun of their ideas or discrediting them, using terms like "That's so stupid," "How in the world can you say that?" or "What have you been smoking?" (unless that statement actually applies). Putting the other person down so you can win the argument might indeed win the argument, but it can result in losing your spouse. Validation encompasses the principle "seek first to understand, then be understood."

You can validate your spouse by asking probing questions and seeking to understand the *why* behind *what* they are saying. By telling your spouse that you honor his feelings and respect his opinion, you validate him and make him feel good about himself. As you validate him, the doors for effective communication will stay open, and constructive dialogue can take place. In any conversation, validation empowers you to connect on an intimate level.

Just as my office lamp plug had to make a connection with the wall socket to work, your conversation has to make a connection with your spouse to work. Care, kindness, and validation provide the electricity that flows between a husband and wife when they connect in conversation. It you start talking together and there is no apparent electricity, then unplug and start again, until it flows! Make that connection, and enjoy meaningful conversation.

Chapter 6

Intimate Conversation

Psychologists have found that couples communicate just as well with strangers as they do with each other. People confuse intimacy with information. Intimacy in conversation is not accomplished by the volume of words spoken or the hours spent talking. My wife always teases me after I play a round of golf with my male friends. She'll ask me what we talked about. I give her the honest answer: "Nothing important." We talk about our bad swing, our horrible putting, and how we'd score better if the course were in better condition—because it's certainly not our fault we are playing so poorly.

She'll say, "You spent five hours together and didn't talk about anything significant or important?"

"Yep." Conversation took place, just not intimacy. And let's be honest, men. Intimacy has no place on the golf course!

Boaz Keysar, a psychology professor and communications expert at the University of Chicago, says, "Closeness can lead people to overestimate how well they communicate."

Epley Nicolas, from the University of Chicago Booth School of Business, says, "Our problem in communicating with friends and spouses is that we have an illusion of insight. Getting close to someone appears to create the *illusion* of understanding more than actual understanding." Couples feel that if they simply "put time in" and say a few interesting things, that deep communication has taken place. Or that if they sit alone on a couch for thirty minutes and have a small chat, that means they've participated in meaningful communication. Talking together takes more than words, proximity or good eye contact. Talking together takes understanding. It takes intimate conversation.

Intimate Conversation for Women

A woman's greatest need is to know that she is loved and cherished above everything and everyone in her husband's life. One of the ways this can be demonstrated is communicating through touch. A woman needs nonsexual affection for her heart to be full. I'll never forget a date night where I went all out to make it a great experience for us. I made reservations for a very nice dinner in a high-end restaurant, took her on a walk downtown, and then watched a chick flick with her. I mean, I went *all* out. A couple days later we were talking, and Autumn told me the highlight of the date night—you know, the "all-out" super-expensive date night. The highlight was when I'd grabbed her hand and held it during the movie. After I did the math in my head on how much money I could have saved on dinner by just holding her hand instead, I realized how different our perspectives were on intimacy. For Autumn it was a simple nonsexual touch that communicated to her that she was mine, that I loved her and wanted to be with her and her alone. Husbands, listen: It's the squeeze of the shoulder, the holding of the hand, the brushing of the face that speaks more of your love than the money you spend. When a husband shows his wife affection, he is sending the message, "I care about you; you are important to me; I am concerned about you as a person I love."

Helen Fisher, author of *Anatomy of Love*, describes why touch is so powerful. "Human skin is like a field of grass, each blade a nerve ending so sensitive that the slightest graze can etch into the human brain a memory of the moment." But what if you, as the husband, are not an affectionate person? Well, if it makes her feel loved, you better become one. Any man can learn to be affectionate. Ask her the type of affection that makes her feel loved. Then purposefully show her the affection that she craves. The payoff is worth the effort many times over. Trust me.

When talking to your wife, get personal, and share with her what you are thinking, doing, and feeling. Men tend to communicate facts. They tend to problem-solve. They tend to grunt and not complete full sentences (tell me I'm wrong). Your wife needs conversation. Honestly, if you'll give her time every day of undivided attention and talking together, your marriage will become more intimate. Share your hopes, dreams, and the things that you are excited about. Talk to her about what hurts you and what is concerning you. Talk about future plans. Thank her for all the things she does for you, for your children, and for others. When you talk together about such things, you are doing more than having a conversation. You're loving her, deeply and intimately. You're touching her soul, her heart, her inner self and filling the need she has for love beyond sex. This type of love is what keeps wives fulfilled and marriages together.

Intimate Conversation for Men

Wives, realize that your husbands are challenged with talking together for the most part. Husbands can't handle too much information at once. Our heads explode easily. So if you have an itemized agenda of ten important things you need to discuss, you might want to consider narrowing that list down to—oh, let's say, *one* thing. Husbands communicate best when one thing is discussed at a time. If Autumn doesn't do this, I get lost in the conversation and check out after a while. But when she stays on topic until we can come to an understanding, then we have a meaningful conversation, and we both feel better.

Save the hours of soul-searching for your girlfriends. Your husband's greatest need is to be respected, affirmed, and encouraged.[1] The greatest gift you can give your husband is words that elevate him and show him respect and dignity. As a wife, you need to see in him what no else can see and to speak that into his life. Your husband needs a wife who is crazy about him and tells him how great he is, even when addressing things he's done that have disappointed or hurt you. Sandwich those comments between words of respect and belief in him and the call of God in his life. When we were first married, Autumn felt an anointing to point out my flaws. Boy, she was gifted at it. But over the first years of marriage, she learned that it was more advantageous to her to become an expert at knowing my strengths (which are many, too innumerable to count, actually). When she talked to me more about my strengths than weaknesses, it helped me to address my weaknesses better, because I didn't feel that my weaknesses were *all* of me. They were *some* of me and could be fixed. But the strengths that Autumn saw in me were who I really was. I was motivated to be confident in them and use them to build our lives together as a husband, father, and breadwinner. This all happened because of words she chose and chooses to speak over me. Proverbs 14:1 says, "The wise woman builds her house, but with her own hands the foolish one tears hers down." The word *hands* is a metaphor representing how a woman's influence can ruin her home. The word *hands* could be replaced with *words*. Words can either build her house up or tear it down. The "wise" woman chooses to build her husband up, using her words as the building materials for a long-lasting marriage. When you talk together with your husband, the right words, at the right time, communicated in the right way can change the trajectory of his life, resulting in a greater destiny.

Enemies of Intimate Conversation

Let's look now at some ugliness in talking together. The following is the Most Wanted List of enemies of intimate conversation.

Angry Words: Anger is an emotion that causes fear in the recipient. And fear escalates emotions up or shuts people down, as they go into protection mode to guard against the hurt of the focused anger. Anger must be controlled and angry words not spoken; they will be damaging. "Don't use foul or abusive language. Let everything you say be good and helpful, so that your words will be an encouragement to those who hear them" (Ephesians 4:29 NLT). This takes self-control. Developing the ability to take control of your thoughts before they become words is critical. Think before you speak. Imagine the future consequences of what you're about to say before you say it. Try to see the future harvest of the seeds you are about to plant, the seeds being your words. A harvest will come. Angry seeds produce an angry harvest.

Insulting Words: Insults suck the life out of your spouse's well-being. We all remember being made fun of in elementary school or junior high. We might have laughed it off, but inside it hurt. Insults are used to bully people into submission by making the insulter seem like the smarter one, the stronger one, the better-looking one, the more deeply spiritual one. Don't insult your spouse into submission as a power play. "Let your conversation be always full of grace, seasoned with salt, so that you may know how to answer everyone" (Colossians 4:6 NIV).

Blame-Shifting: A mature person takes responsibility for his or her mistakes. Blaming others is the response of someone who is insecure and immature. Don't blame your spouse for something that they didn't do or say. This puts them in a defensive posture, and you won't be able to have a positive, productive conversation. Blame-shifting didn't work for Adam, and it won't work for you either.

Hijacking the Conversation: Talking together requires the *together* part. A one-sided conversation is only fun for the person doing all the talking. Don't dominate the conversation by talking too much, talking over your spouse, or by not listening. "A truly wise person uses few words; a person with understanding is even-tempered" (Proverbs 17:27 NLT). Be a ready listener when it's time to talk together. Make sure your thoughts are formulated and that your words will bring life to the conversation. "A fool does not think before he unleashes his temper, but a wise man holds back and remains quiet" (Proverbs 29:11 The Voice). Talk less, and listen more.

Lack of Empathy: Empathy means putting yourself in the other person's position, trying to feel what he feels and see what he sees, and attempting to understand where he is coming from. Lack of empathy destroys intimate conversation when the person sharing his heart feels misunderstood or feels a disconnect and a lack of feeling from the listening spouse. This is translated as, "She doesn't really care, and so forget about it. I'm done talking."

Not Talking Face to Face: This is a big one. As mentioned, 60 percent of communication is body language. More is said by the way you position your body and facial expression than by the words you use. This is why there is a lack in digital communication.

Emails and texts have the words, but they lack the spirit of intent that is communicated through body language. I understand in this day and age that phones are now used widely for communication, but when something is really serious, I recommend getting in a room and having a face-to-face conversation.

You can see that talking together can be a bit complex before meaningful conversation takes place. I encourage you to review the chapters of this section of the book and make a list of the things that you need to improve on in your talking-together skills. What do you need to do better? What do you need to do more of? What adjustments to your daily schedule do you need to make so you can create time to talk together? Any changes will be an improvement, and any improvement will add life to your marriage.

Part Three

Deciding Together

Chapter 7

That Little Thing Called Unity

I love bold colors. Autumn loves boring neutral colors—sorry, I mean neutral colors. Our home had white walls. I needed some color in order to survive. So one weekend while she was out of town, I thought I would surprise her. I painted the downstairs bathroom a dark burgundy color. Brilliant move on my part. And by the way, do you know how much work it is to paint bathrooms? She returned from her trip, saw the color, and was absolutely speechless—just not in the way I had hoped. Her first words after she collected herself were a demand that I paint it white again right away. The good news? I became really good at painting bathrooms.

The painting story illustrates one of many big decisions I personally made in the first ten years of our marriage that I didn't consult my wife on first. I regretted those decisions every time. I didn't want the hassle of discussing them, arguing over them, or facing up to the fact that she wouldn't support what I wanted to do. So my conclusion was, why even ask? Those decisions cost us money, time, and heartache. The worst ramification, though, was the divide it put between me and my wife. With her help, I began to see how immature I was in this regard. I saw how selfish I was and how much distrust I had toward Autumn. As a result of my inclination to make big decisions on my own, she no longer trusted me. She lived in insecurity and fear. What would I do next? What would I buy next? What risk would I assume next? It was a rough time for us.

One day, my friend Steve was going to buy a new television, and he invited me to the electronics store to help him pick one out. What guy doesn't want to go to the electronics store with his friend and look at TVs? Can you guess what I brought home? A brand-new TV, purchased without Autumn's blessing or knowledge. I wasn't planning on buying one—until I saw the sale and *had to have it*. And boy, did Autumn *let me have it*—not the TV but her displeasure at my selfish, unwise ways.

I finally saw the problem I had. It took a while after the TV episode, but I eventually realized that I needed Autumn by my side in all decisions of consequence. We were a couple. I needed her input, wisdom, and perspective. I had to realize that it was better for us to make decisions together rather than me making them alone.

The Bible talks about the blessing of unity within families. Psalms 133:1–3 says: "Behold, how good and pleasant it is when brothers dwell in unity. It is like the precious oil on the head, running down on the beard, on the beard of Aaron, running down on the collar of his robes! It is like the dew of Hermon which falls on the mountains of Zion! For there the Lord has commanded the blessing, life forevermore" (ESV). The phrase "brothers dwelling together" appears in Genesis 13:6 and 36:7 in reference to large families whose livestock wouldn't fit in one location anymore. There was potential for family strife unless they could dwell together in unity. The lands mentioned in these passages were fruitful lands of blessing and prosperity. But all of that was at risk due to anger and strife within these families. When strife, disagreement, and disunity begin to outgrow the blessing of unity in marriage, then one spouse eventually feels there isn't room for him or her anymore in the marriage. Unity ensures that there is always room for both spouses to live in the land of blessing. Unified couples commit to working things out, to solve problems together, and to change what needs to be changed in order to maintain unity. This results in living in a "land of blessing." Husbands and wives dwelling in unity under the blessing of the covenant of marriage are truly living in the land of blessing.

David likens living in unity to precious oil poured on Aaron's head and running down his beard. Aaron was the high priest in Israel. One of his responsibilities was that he alone entered the Holy of Holies on the Day of Atonement to offer the sacrifices for the whole nation, expiating their sin. So much oil was poured over Aaron that it ran down his beard. In the Bible, oil represents the presence of the Holy Spirit. The Holy Spirit wants to pour himself over our marriages. Aaron's anointing resulted in his being able to fulfill his role as high priest. When couples invite the Holy Spirit to pour himself on their marriages, this then enables them to fulfill their roles as husband and wife. The precious oil of the Holy Spirit brings the land of blessing to our marriages, and we will be able to dwell there, together, until death do us part. The Holy Spirit helps us to deal with the challenges we'll face, without one of us feeling that he can't "dwell" here anymore.

David goes on and declares that unity in relationships is like the dew of Hermon. Mount Hermon is a mountain range in north Palestine. At 9,200 feet above sea level, it is the highest mountain peak in the area. Because of the height, the mountaintop is snowcapped for up to nine months a year. The melted snow pack is a major water source for the Jordan River. What David is writing about is the periodic currents of cool air that would carry moisture to the surrounding lowlands as they made their way down to Jerusalem. This moisture would help the crops grow, causing the land to be blessed with a large harvest. The *dew of Hermon* represents refreshment and growth. The cool currents brought a feeling of relief from drought conditions.

Drought seasons can refer to times of stress, hunger, and anxiety. Without unity, marriages can suffer drought conditions. Husbands and wives don't grow together but instead grow apart, resulting in separate lives. Stress sets in. Hunger for life-giving relationships leads to inappropriate emotional affairs with others, who feed the need for human connection that is lacking in the marriage. Anxiety about whether the marriage will make it through the storm sets in, and the makings for a miserable marriage are present. The dew of Hermon brought growth to crops and provided nourishment for the people of Israel. The dew of unity in marriage brings relief from relational drought and nourishes the marriage, causing husbands and wives to grow in their relationship. David is making the point that unity in relationships brings blessings and a fruitful harvest. How good and pleasant it is when married couples can dwell together in unity in the land of blessing. Let's look a bit deeper into this little thing called unity and learn some practical steps to deciding together.

Chapter 8

Steps to Deciding Together

Married couples always have big decisions to make, from what to buy, to how much to spend on things, to where to eat, where to live, what church to attend, and how on earth to raise those kids. I want to give you seven steps that can assist you in the process of deciding together.

Step One: Take your time. The first step is to never make a big decision quickly. Big decisions have big consequences. Big decisions affect other people, like your family members. Big decisions put finances at risk. Big decisions can alter a career trajectory, a ministry path, or a child's future. That's why they're called *big* decisions. When faced with a big decision, do not make it quickly. Take time to pray about it. Take time to think about it. Take time to sleep on it. Take time to look at the pros and cons, trying to see and predict the potential outcomes. Take time to seek counsel from wise people who have no stake in the decision one way or another, so they can give you unvarnished opinions. Once you've looked at all the information and have sought the Lord's wisdom in prayer, follow the peace you feel about what to do.

Peace is the key way that God gives us direction on what to do. When you have peace about what decision to make, you simply understand that you know what to do, and you both feel good about it. If there is agreement between the two of you, then you need to seek out unity and confirmation from two or three other people. Confirmation from others is a Biblical principle worth implementing into the decision-making process. In Deuteronomy 19:15, Moses is rehearsing God's law with Israel and writes this, "A matter must be established by the testimony of two or three witnesses." This verse relates directly to convicting someone of a crime, but the principle of confirmation applies to a wide variety of necessary decisions. Jesus even quoted this verse in Matthew 18:16 when teaching on how to confront and correct people in the church. It's worth bringing your matter up to people whose wisdom and opinion you respect. They just might save you the pain of making a bad decision on your own.

When you are at peace with your decision, you are able to sleep at night. You are excited about the decision. Others are excited for you. Paul writes in 1 Corinthians 14:33: "For God is not a God of confusion but of peace" (ESV). When in doubt, don't do it. It's not worth the pain, sorrow, and problems a bad big decision brings. Years ago I had a big opportunity presented to me. It was with a man I didn't know well, but he had a good reputation. The opportunity required a big decision—actually, it was a huge decision. I shared it with my wife. Together we prayed over it. I sought counsel from wise men who knew this man well and got their opinions. I looked at the pros and cons. It took six months to come to a place of peace. All the lights turned green, and I pursued the opportunity. It was not only a big decision but a good one.

On the other hand, when I was a young youth pastor of a successful youth ministry, the lead pastor who'd hired me had left to pastor another church, and the new pastor wanted to bring in his own youth pastor, so I was let go. Autumn and I moved back to my hometown, and I looked for a job until another ministry opportunity would open up. Well, I got a job selling floor covering. I was doing well with it but didn't like it. I was a pastor, for goodness' sake. I was twenty-eight at the time and thought I could make my own way. So I decided to start a public school-assembly speaking ministry. As a youth pastor, I knew that schools paid pretty good money for speakers to come in and address the student body in an assembly. I myself had brought some guys in to speak at the schools in my city, as a matter of fact, and I knew I could do it too. So I put together a school-assembly program called "Real Issues," which was a talk on values. I would come and speak to students about valuing themselves, valuing others, and valuing their future. I'd hit all the hot-button issues of teen suicide, drug and alcohol use, violence, racism, and the importance of doing well in school. It all came together in a nice package. I was pumped. But before I launched it officially, I asked for a breakfast meeting with a wise businessman, to get his counsel on the business side of things. He considered it a risky venture but thought that if anyone could do something like this, I could. I was encouraged. But there was a part of his counsel I didn't like. He told me it would take three years for this venture to support me financially, so not to quit my current job yet. I did not want to hear that. I was so ready to quit selling carpet, linoleum, and floor tiles. It was a big decision. I made the wrong one. Without consulting my wife, I quit my job and launched into this new venture. Against the wise businessman's counsel, I took out a loan and borrowed against our savings to fund my new start-up. Well, schools did hire me. I spoke that year to ten thousand students. But that was not enough money to fund our family (my wife was a stay-at-home mom with three small children at the time). The money ran out before I had enough momentum to keep Real Issues going full time. I eventually had to use our savings to pay back the loan and count it as a loss. It was a costly quick decision. Quick decisions rarely work out well. So take all the time necessary to get to the place where the decision is easy to make.

Step 2: Set aside adequate time to talk about the decision. Deciding together takes talking together, as we discussed in the last section. Set aside plenty of time to thoroughly talk through every angle, every possibility, every aspect of the decision. Choose a quiet place. Talk together in a location where the atmosphere promotes intimate conversation. And talk until you can't talk about it anymore, until you come together in unity. Oh, and go back and read chapters 4 to 6 again as a review on how to talk together.

Step 3: Communicate your position clearly. Deciding together takes understanding on both sides. If you as a couple disagree about something you are trying to decide together, make sure you are able to communicate your position clearly. It's helpful to organize your thoughts ahead of time. Write down the *what, why, who, when, how,* and *how much,* and read them if necessary. In other words, know your position before you start to talk. Answer the following, and communicate the answers to your spouse:

What do I want to do?

Why do I want to do this?

Who is involved in this decision, and who would be affected by it?

When should this happen?

How would this happen?

How much is this going to cost?

It's also important to submit your ideas to your spouse. Use terms like "I want to submit an idea for you to consider with me," or "I'd like to get your opinion on something I've been thinking about." If a spouse just says, "Here's what we're going to do," or "I've decided to take this plan of action," then it leaves the other spouse feeling helpless. The decision has already been made, and if the other spouse speaks up, an argument ensues. Deciding together takes, well, deciding *together*. This shows mutual respect and partnership.

Step 4: Don't get defensive. Defensiveness shuts down communication. Walls go up, hearts get hard, and talking together stops. When your spouse disagrees with you on something, you need to open your heart to listen and let him explain his position. Otherwise, division comes, and a bad decision is made. After you state your position, ask your spouse to share his feelings, thoughts and opinions. Be open to a different point of view. It's important to let him finish his thoughts without cutting him off midsentence. That would show a lack of respect and disregard for his position. Defensiveness is a killer to decision making.

Step 5: Validate your spouse's feelings if they are different than yours. It's okay for both of you to look at a decision that needs to be made and see it differently. That is actually healthy. You need to look at decisions from all angles. Multiple perspectives give clarity and logic to the decision. Remember that all decisions have consequences, either good or bad. So when your spouse sees things differently, validate her feelings and take her opinion under consideration. Nothing shows a person she is valued more than being validated by those around her. It doesn't mean she is right in her perspective. What it means is that you support her as a valuable member of the marriage partnership and are interested in what she has to say. Validation responses would be, "I can see why you might feel that way," "I understand your concern. Here is my response to your concern." And then Step 6 begins.

Step 6: Begin the process of the "back and forth." This is where the discussion regarding the decision gets real. Your spouse has made his opinion known about the decision at hand. You've responded to his opinion, and your response is different than what he had hoped for. But he has validated your opinion, because he values you as his spouse. So now begins the *rumble*. The "back and forth" is the discussion in which you try to overcome the differences of opinion and obtain unity so you can move forward. This is where opportunities for *truth spoken in love* appear. This is the moment when Galatians 5:22 is tested. Is this conversation going to be filled with *love, joy, peace, patience, kindness, goodness, faithfulness, gentleness, and self-control?* Be sure to guard your emotions during what can be a volatile conversation. Guard against anger, sarcasm, yelling, and a dominating spirit. Things can escalate quickly when emotions catch fire. It's important to remember that you're looking to make a joint decision that will be beneficial to your family. Allow time for your partner to speak and respond. Look for the areas in which compromise can be reached. If after the back-and-forth phase you can reach unity and agreement on the decision, then move forward and enjoy the results.

But …

Step 7: If you can't come to unity in the decision, stop the discussion before damaging anger and frustration set in. This is when a time out and time away from each other is healthy. If you just can't find common ground, then it's best to realize you are stuck and it would be best to elicit outside counsel. It's okay to "agree to disagree" at this moment, just as long as you also agree to delay making the decision until you can come together again and decide together. While apart, take time to pray and ask God, What is the best decision? What is the best strategy?

What is the best outcome that can be achieved? Then arrange to get wisdom and input from someone on the outside—preferably mutual counsel from someone who is not affected by the decision one way or another. It should be someone you both agree on. If it's a financial decision, find someone who is really good with money. If it's a parenting decision, find people who have had success raising their kids who can share with you from their experience. If it's a spiritual decision regarding church or ministry, find someone who has walked that path before and seek his advice. Autumn and I were faced with a big decision when we were young parents, in regard to our strong-willed firstborn daughter. When she was four, she was defiant, and she terrorized us as young parents. We had to decide how to handle her in the area of discipline and rebellion that was beginning to show. I had an opinion and Autumn had an opinion. We were at opposite ends of the child-discipline spectrum. So we sought advice from a couple in our church who had raised five children successfully. That meeting changed our lives. We adopted their advice and decided together to discipline our children according to what they taught us. It was difficult, but we stuck with it because we were in agreement that it was the best decision for our daughter. As we implemented the decision we made regarding discipline, our daughter began to change and became loving, sweet, and obedient. She grew to be a wonderful teenager and is now a great wife and mother who is involved in our church. Take the "time out" needed to get help in deciding together.

Here are a couple of final thoughts. Husbands, listen to your wives. Woman sense things that men don't always sense, especially when it comes to financial and family matters. Always submit your ideas to them and listen to their responses. I was horrible at this as a young husband. I was bold, confident, and not afraid of risk. Yet I lacked good judgment at times. I failed often and made mistakes that hurt my marriage and my finances. When I began listening to my wife and learning the value of unity, my life changed for the better. Autumn has saved me from myself multiple times by helping me see the error of my ideas, the risk that was too costly to take, and the timing that was bad. And I love her for it.

Wives, trust your husbands on certain decisions involving risk. Men are risk takers. God created us that way. It's in a man's nature to risk, to seize the opportunity, to build, to pursue, to rise to a challenge, and to provide. Yes, I've talked about the downside of risk in my own experience. But there are times when Autumn realizes that what I am presenting is something I need to do, and she assumes the risk alongside me. Hard as it has been for her, she has seen the rewards of taking risk; it has paid off because we did it together. A husband will at times want to take an adventure in life, regarding his career or financial investment, that involves a certain amount of risk. Sometimes you have to let him go. There is a balance here. If the decision is a guaranteed train wreck, then stand your ground and help him to see your side. But if the risk isn't foolish or certain to fail, then trust God in your husband, pray for him and his venture, and go along for the ride. Risk often pays off in big ways when it works out in the end. Success in life as a couple is the result of making good decisions—together.

Part Four

Fighting Together

Chapter 9

The Cause of Conflict in Marriage

"What causes quarrels and what causes fights among you? Is it not this, that your passions are at war within you? You desire and do not have, so you murder. You covet and cannot obtain, so you fight and quarrel. You do not have, because you do not ask. You ask and do not receive, because you ask wrongly, to spend it on your passions" (James 4:1-3 ESV).

James, who many scholars believe was the half-brother of Jesus and pastor of the church in Jerusalem, is writing this letter to Christians in his church. He had to address many issues in the lives of his congregation, and one that he addressed in chapter 4 is conflict between people. The Greek word he used in verse 1, for quarrels, is *pomelos*, which means "war, a battle, a clash." James uses another strong word in verse 1, for fights. The Greek word for fights is *"mache"*, which means "an intense, bitter battle." James was about to address some serious, intense, bitter conflict issues. In our counseling of married couples, Autumn and I have seen many sessions that included *pomelos* and *mache*—bitter, intense battles between husbands and wives that seem insolvable.

The Causes of Conflict

The first cause of conflict that James writes about are the "passions" that are "at war" within us. James asks a rhetorical question, "What causes *pomelos* and *mache?*" He then gives the answer, which is "your passions are at war within you." The Greek word for passions is *hedone,* which is the word the English hedonism comes from. Hedonism means "pleasure." James is saying that unbridled passion, or desire for what *we* want, for what would bring *us* pleasure, is the root cause of conflict. We *want* something so badly that if our spouses stand in our way then we will *fight* to get it.

The second cause of conflict James gives is in verse 2: "you desire but do not have." Unfulfilled desire causes conflict in marriage. A wife can experience disappointment in her husband because he isn't able to financially provide material desires or even her basic needs. A husband can be disappointed in his wife's refusal to explore sexual desires he has. A wife may desire more alone time and quality conversation with her husband, but he doesn't take the time or engage in talking together, to her disappointment. A husband may have a desire to share his interest in sports, motorcycles, hunting, or building things, but the wife may simply not be interested in those things and refuse to play along. When a spouse desires from his partner something that brings pleasure and doesn't get it, the passions come out, and fighting ensues.

The third cause of conflict is also found in verse 2. James writes, "you covet and cannot obtain." To covet is to desire something you shouldn't have, like someone else's wife or husband or the single guy or girl at work. A person can also covet a house, car, or boat that they can't afford. People can create and live in fantasy worlds of material things or human relationships that they can't have, and it causes conflict and fighting in a relationship. Desiring something you can't have, or shouldn't have, is dangerous. It causes frustration, envy, jealousy, and other ugly things you don't want in your marriage. The opposite of coveting is being content. Contentment is keeping your desires within the boundaries of what you already have. Paul writes to Timothy that contentment is a wonderful thing, "But godliness with contentment is great gain, for we brought nothing into the world, and we cannot take anything out of the world. But if we have food and clothing, with these we will be content" (1 Timothy 6:6–8 ESV). Paul goes on, in verses 9 and 10, to describe what can happen to someone who covets. They will fall into temptation, into a snare or trap and into many senseless and harmful desires that will bring people into ruin and destruction. *Wow!* I vote for contentment. When a spouse brings discontentment into a marriage, destruction can follow in the form of ugly fights, financial debt, and the risk of emotional or even sexual affairs. It's important that you check covetousness at the door and adopt an attitude of gratefulness for all you do have.

The key here is to guard your heart from coveting things or people that you can't have. Be content with where you are in life and with what you *can* have.

The fourth cause of conflict James mentions in verse 2 is lack of communication. "You do not have, because you do not ask." In the context of James 4, many scholars think he is referring to prayer here, asking God for what we need instead of relying on others. I would agree. But for our discussion here, I would like to use this principle in the context of marriage. Conflict comes when we don't communicate to our partners what our needs, expectations, or desires are. We assume our spouses will "get it" without our having to tell them, as if they are mind readers and should just know our thoughts without us having to verbally express them. When what we think should happen doesn't happen, conflict arises, as we get angry, disappointed, or frustrated.

To get what you want you have to ask for it. You have to communicate (out loud) to your spouse what you would like to have. I might want a chocolate ice cream sundae for dessert tonight. (In fact, I *do* want a hot chocolate sundae tonight—I'd better tell her!) If I don't ask for one, then I'm not going to get one. If I don't communicate to Autumn that it would great if she would make one for me after dinner, then odds are I'll be looking at an empty bowl of nothing. I can get angry and yell. I can belittle her. I can express how frustrated I am because she's not meeting my needs. But it would all be in vain if I never verbally expressed to her my desire for one in the first place.

You can't expect something from your husband that you haven't asked for. Many birthdays and anniversaries have been ruined because of unmet expectations over non-communicated desires. How was he supposed to know you wanted to go the beach for a few days for your twenty-fifth anniversary if you never mentioned it? What do you mean, he was just supposed to know? One thing I know about most men is that they don't know *anything* about what is in a woman's head. Men, why would you expect your wife to automatically go where you want to go sexually if you don't communicate with her? Save yourself some grief, and communicate openly and often about what you want. If you'll do this, the odds of you getting it will greatly increase!

Lastly, the fifth cause of conflict in James 1 is in verse 3, "you ask and do not receive because you ask wrongly." Along the same lines as cause number 4, which is not asking at all, you can ask "wrongly." Asking wrongly has to do with motive and attitude. If you are asking with a motive to manipulate or with a bad, negative attitude, your spouse will not want to give you what you desire.

If your attitude is demanding, dominating, or disrespectful, your spouse will refuse to give you want you want. Or if she does give it to you, it's with a heart that feels forced into it, and not with a heart of joy that she is getting to bless you with something important to you. Use words like "please" or descriptive phrases like "you know what would be fun for me," "you know what I'd really like to do," or similar expressions that come across in a positive, life-giving way. Being appreciative that she would even consider your request goes a long way. Submitting an idea and getting her take on it is a great way to come to agreement. Demanding the salt shaker is way less appealing than asking nicely. If you want to ask and receive, then ask "rightly." Asking rightly will reap many more "receives" on your behalf.

We've looked at some of the passions that rise up out of us and cause conflict in marriage. Now let's look at some ways that we hurt each other when in conflict.

Chapter 10

How We Hurt Each Other
when We Fight

When I was ten years old, I was visiting my cousin's house in the woods of Mill Valley, California, a community outside of San Francisco. Right behind his house was a forest with big redwoods and trails to hike on. So off we went on a big adventure. He was a couple of years older than me, so I looked up to him; I thought he was the coolest guy ever. He and his older brothers had pet snakes, cool cars, and big muscles. I was related to awesomeness. So when my cousin invited me to go on a wild adventure in the woods, I was ready, especially because he was going to take along a big-bladed hunting knife he had just received as a gift. The blade was so shiny and sharp. I couldn't wait to see if he would let me hold it.

Off we went. I soon found out that we weren't going to just hike on a ready-made parks and recreation trail; we were going to clear our own trail. I loved watching him cut branches and bushes with that knife. I wanted to try it. So I asked him if I could hold the knife and cut some stuff. He said yes, and as I reached out my hand to take the knife, he decided to take one more swing with it, and my hand accidentally got in the way. The blade went into my right-hand index finger next to the middle joint. The cut went deep, and the blood starting pouring. I freaked, and we both started running back to the house. My parents drove me to the hospital and I ended up with seven stitches in my finger. Luckily there was no permanent damage to my finger, and I have full mobility and use of it. As I write this, I'm looking at my finger and seeing the big scar that starts in the middle of the inside of my finger and wraps around the joint to the middle of the outside of my finger, a constant reminder of the wound I suffered many years ago. At ten years old, I got over the trauma pretty quickly. In fact, my cousin and I went back in the woods and collected all the leaves lying on the ground that had my blood on them. So cool.

There are many ways husbands and wives hurt each other when fighting. And those hurts can leave permanent scars on our emotions, much like the scar on my finger. I may have suffered the wound a long time ago, but the scar still exists—the memory, the emotion, the fear. Often the wounds come during a fight, when emotions are high, words aren't filtered, and anger lashes out like the knife in my cousin's hand. Let's look at some of the ways couples hurt each other when they fight.

We hurt each other by blaming. Blame is when we hold the other person totally responsible for the situation. Blame allows the accusing spouse to be free from any responsibility whatsoever. The blamer gives himself license to pile on without mercy, making the offending spouse bear the whole burden alone.

We hurt each other by accusing. This occurs when a husband, for example, brings an allegation of wrongdoing to his wife without proof. Or a wife might find a receipt to a restaurant and come to the conclusion that her husband is having an affair, when really she has no solid proof, just an allegation based on a receipt. What accusation does is to wipe out trust. When trust is missing in a marriage, there is nothing left to build a relationship on. When a spouse incorrectly accuses the other of wrongdoing without proof, then the accused spouse will be on the defensive constantly. He will feel watched, not trusted, and be walking on eggshells in regard to the relationship. He'll feel bound by the accusing spouse and feel as if he has to justify every move he makes. I know of a husband whose wife suspects him without any burden of proof. He claims to have done nothing wrong. His wife makes him text her whenever he changes his location, and she wants him to activate his phone tracker so she can follow his every move. All this is without reason, except fear and suspicion. That is no way for a spouse to live and no way for a marriage to grow. There has to be a great level of trust in order for couples to grow strong and for marriages to last.

We hurt each other by lying. If couples deliberately say things that are untrue to each other, then as with accusation, trust is broken. Trust broken by lies is very hard to restore. It takes time; it takes proving yourself; it takes the long process of rebuilding that bond.

We hurt each other by resenting. This comes about when one spouse has ill feelings toward the other that are so negative they don't even want to be in the same room with him or her. To tell someone you resent them is saying that you don't even want to be in the same room with him or her. Resentment is such a strong negative feeling that to possess it can harm a person's health. It's the closest thing to hatred that a spouse can feel.

We hurt each other by yelling. No doubt voices being raised can be part of a couple's fighting process. But there is a line that gets crossed when a raised voice turns into yelling and screaming.

Yelling is used as a way to dominate people and intimidate them into submission. People in a state of yelling are never in the mood to compromise, to understand, or to listen well for the purpose of coming to agreement. It's all-out war at this point.

We hurt each other by labelling. This is when one spouse uses a descriptive word to describe the other spouse. I'm not talking about a cute nickname that shows love and affection. I'm talking about a slur, a slander, or a hurtful label that attacks character and demeans them. *Lazy, liar, useless,* and *stupid* are labels that sting and stick with a person, harming self-esteem and, even worse, deadening the feelings of the recipient toward the spouse using them.

We hurt each other by reliving past failures. Couples who constantly remind each other of their past failures use this as a weapon to bring harm. It's hard to forget the past, to leave the past behind. It takes maturity to give people time to change and to believe that they have. Fighting should be about the present situation, about the solution to the problem, and looking to the future. Just as God doesn't hold our past over our heads, we shouldn't do that to our spouses.

We hurt each other by insulting. This is when couples use offensive words that cut deep. Insults embarrass, ridicule, humiliate, and tear down.

We hurt each other by invalidating. Invalidation means showing how the other person is wrong in a mean and hurtful way. "You're so stubborn—why can't you see how wrong you are?" "Are you crazy? How can you possibly think that will work?" Invalidation adds insult to injury by stacking negative comments on top of each other.

We hurt each other by exaggerating. This means to overstate something and make it more noticeable or make it appear larger than it really is. When you magnify the problem by exaggeration, it makes your spouse more at fault then he or she really is. This is the territory of *"you always"* and *"you never."* These statements are usually overstatements used to exaggerate the size or frequency of the problem.

We hurt each other by physically attacking. Physical attack is using physical violence to cause harm. This is a line that should never be crossed. If it is being crossed, then you need to seek professional help immediately. Physical attack or abuse should never be tolerated under any circumstance.

This is a list of the deadly inner weapons at your disposal when you fight together. You must be careful and use self-control so you never pick them up to use them. Lock them in your inner-weapons safe and throw away the key. The hurts from this list can take years to heal. Some never do. Trust me, you don't want the responsibility for being the one who inflicted irreparable damage to your spouse. Many couples live with deep regret over things that were said and done in the heat of fighting together. The worst part is that most of the time things were said that they didn't really mean, but in order to "win" or make a "point" for their side, they crossed over into using weapons that scarred.

Are there ways to fight without causing lasting scars or negative impact on your marriage? I believe that, yes, there are. Let's look at some ways to make it a positive experience when you fight together.

Chapter 11

How to Fight Together and Win

We've covered some causes of conflict as well as ways that couples hurt each other when they fight. Let me now give you principles that will help you fight effectively and come out the other end stronger as a couple, instead of weaker.

James, who gave us the causes of conflict we covered in chapter 9, also gives us wisdom and insights on how to work through conflict. Let's look at what he wrote. "My dear brothers and sisters, take note of this: Everyone should be quick to listen, slow to speak, and slow to become angry, because human anger does not produce the righteousness that God desires (James 1:19–20 NIV)."

The first principle James gives is to "be quick to listen." Listening is a learned skill. It comes naturally easier to some than it does to others. Good listeners live in the moment. They focus solely on the person who is talking. And good listeners empathize. Empathy is trying to feel for yourself what the other is feeling. If the other is sad, empathy brings a twinge of sadness to you to as you try to put yourself in her position. If she is discouraged, then you try to imagine the discouragement she is feeling, not for the sake of staying there but for the sake of helping bring her out of it. But first there must be an empathetic emotional connection between the two of you. This will result in the person speaking feeling valued, which will allow her to move forward with the issues at hand. If good listening doesn't take place during a disagreement, then a couple will get stuck in the mud of frustration and may never get out. It takes listening to bring resolution and reconciliation.

Second, James advises to "be slow to speak." In other words, *think* before you speak. Do your best to calculate the impact of your words. Is what you're about to say going to help or hurt the situation? Is what you are about to say going to help or hurt your spouse? Will your words add fuel to the fire or bring fresh water to put the fire out? Rash outbursts of negative words will bring death. Overreaction and destructive criticism result when you are not slow to speak but allow quick, reactionary verbal outbursts. Being slow to speak takes a certain maturity. Holding your tongue is a tough thing to do at times. We've all been there. So when things start to get heated, take a moment to pause, take a couple deep breaths, and use wisdom in deciding whether what you're about to say will be worth it. Hearts can be permanently scarred from negative words spoken rashly. "I didn't mean it" doesn't take the pain away. It's better not to say it.

Third, James counsels us to "be slow to anger." Anger is an interesting emotion, because it can do so much good when it's focused on eradicating evil and injustice. It was anger that caused David to make a run at Goliath and take him out, because he insulted God. It was anger that caused William Wilberforce to battle the British slave trade for twenty-six years before the eventual passage of the Slave Trade Act of 1807. It was anger that stirred up Dr. Martin Luther King and the other leaders of the Civil Rights Movement to bring an end to racial segregation and discrimination. Anger stirred Jesus up to overturn the tables in the temple courtyard where commerce was taking place instead of worship and prayer. Rightly placed anger can lead to very good things. But it can also cause much damage when it's focused on hurting the ones we love.

Anger is a biological reaction that affects our emotions when we feel hurt, at risk, violated, or mistreated. A person uses anger to deflect pain or the fear of pain coming. It's a defense mechanism. Anger is caused by something that threatens us.

In marriage anger is triggered by unmet expectations, lies, disappointments, disunity, financial mistrust, unfaithfulness, insecurity, and many other things. In reality, anger is part of life and marriage. It must by understood and managed.

Anger is mentioned in the Bible around 350 times and usually in a negative context.

Proverbs 22:24–25 (NLT): "Don't befriend angry people or associate with hot-tempered people, or you will learn to be like them and endanger your soul."

Proverbs 27:4 (NLT): "Anger is cruel and wrath is like a flood."

Proverbs 29:22 (NLT): "An angry person starts fights; a hot-tempered person commits all kinds of sin."

Ephesians 4:26–27 (NLT): And "don't sin by letting anger control you." Don't let the sun go down while you are still angry, for anger gives a foothold to the devil.

1 Timothy 2:8 (NLT): "In every place of worship, I want men to pray with holy hands lifted up to God, free from anger and controversy."

The key to keeping anger in check is self-control. When anger begins to rear its ugly head, self-control looks like this:

- Recognition. You feel it coming, and so you begin to shut things down for a bit until the anger subsides.
- Walking away. Take some time away from each other to cool off.

- Breathe deeply. Deep breathing is very real form of relaxation. It takes the edge off and allows your blood flow to slow down, your adrenaline levels to lower, and your thoughts to clear.
- Prayer. After walking away and breathing deeply, take time to pray and ask for God's guidance, wisdom, and help in finding the solution to this disagreement.
- Worship. Listening to worship music does something to our souls. It calms our emotions and brings God's presence, if our hearts are open.

Fourth, James doesn't mention this, but it is a major theme in the Bible. We are to offer and receive *forgiveness*. The hardest four words for a person to say are "Will you forgive me?" Why is that? It's because asking for forgiveness takes an incredible amount of humility, which for most of us is in short supply. We love to think that we are the ones who are right, not at fault, and victims. We are convinced our spouses are wrong; it's their fault, and they are the ones who are causing us to suffer.

For a fight to come to a productive conclusion, forgiveness must be offered and received by both husband and wife. Asking your spouse to forgive you is much more powerful than simply offering an apology and saying, "I'm sorry." When you tell your spouse you're sorry, he isn't required to give anything back to you. The best response he can give is the trite and meaningless verbal response, "Okay. I'm glad you're sorry. Don't do it again." But he has given nothing from the heart in return. It's simply a response to a statement. But when you ask someone, "Will you forgive me?" then you require a heart response back. It's the heart response that changes things. When you ask "Will you forgive me?" it gives your spouse the opportunity to give you the gift of forgiveness. This heart response is good for both you and your spouse. By asking "Will you forgive me?" you humble yourself and admit you were wrong and want to make things right. You also give your spouse an opportunity to do the same in return. To forgive someone also takes humility, so by offering, giving, and receiving forgiveness, husbands and wives soften their hearts toward one another, they achieve togetherness, and they can move forward from the conflict.

It needs to be said that bestowing forgiveness is an option. The person offended or hurt does not have to say, "I forgive you." He or she has the choice to stay angry, hurt, or bitter. Also, if you are the person asking for forgiveness and your spouse refuses, it's important to know that before God, you've done your part. Your responsibility is to humble yourself, say you're sorry, and give your spouse the opportunity to forgive you by asking for it. If she refuses to grant forgiveness, then she will suffer the consequences mentioned above. Her anger will remain, she will continue to feel hurt, and bitterness will grow. That is an issue she will have to deal with if she wants to receive healing and restoration in her marriage.

Forgiveness is gift, a gift that must be offered freely, with no conditions, obligations, or expectations. *Forgiveness* is a term used to indicate a pardon for a fault or offense. It excuses from payment for a debt owed.[1] Jesus modeled giving the gift of forgiveness better than anyone—from forgiving the adulterous woman in John 8, to forgiving those responsible for nailing him to the cross in Luke 23:34, to granting us forgiveness every time we confess our sins in 1 John 1:9. Through forgiveness, Jesus released people who hurt him, rejected him, and mocked him from guilt and shame over their wrongs. Forgiveness is a powerful force that *always* brings life into relationships, both our relationships with Jesus and our human relationships—and especially our marriages.

Forgiveness is achieved when you lift and carry away someone's sin against you. It's taking the guilt your spouse feels after he has hurt you and carrying it away from him, relieving him from the guilt and shame of his mistakes or wrongdoing.

I know of someone who was hit hard during the financial collapse of 2008. He was laid off from his job and lost his house to foreclosure. After the foreclosure, the bank settled with him for six cents on the dollar. He was able to afford to pay the bank what they were asking and walk away from the rest, totally forgiven by the bank. The bank allowed him to walk away from the burden of the debt he carried, by showing mercy and extending forgiveness for the majority of the debt he owed. Forgiving someone is taking the burden he is carrying from hurting you and carrying it away from him.

In 2 Corinthians 5:18–20, Paul writes about the dynamics of reconciliation. "All this is from God, who reconciled us to himself through Christ and gave us the ministry of reconciliation: that God was reconciling the world to himself in Christ, not counting people's sins against them. And he has committed to us the message of reconciliation" (NIV).

I like to apply the same principle to marriage. As husbands and wives, we have the task of reconciling our relationships to each other. When people reconcile with God, it's through his forgiveness of their sins. When married couples reconcile, it's through forgiving each other for the sins, hurts, and violations they've committed against each other. Long-term marriages are possible through a series of numerous reconciliation moments, during which hearts are softened, forgiveness is asked for, forgiveness is granted, and they then move forward, leaving that conflict behind.

Drs. Les and Leslie Parrott wrote in their book, *The Good Fight*[2] that a good apology involves three Rs. They are Responsibility: "I know I hurt your feelings." Regret: "I feel terrible that I hurt you." Remedy: "I won't do it again."

I would add one more thing to the list, even though it doesn't start with R—Forgiveness: "Would you forgive me?"

As we end this chapter, remember that you and your spouse are on the same team. One of the reasons couples stray apart during and after a fight is that they view each other as an enemy. When you are fighting an enemy, you are out to destroy that person. You will do or say anything to win. Why? Because you don't care about the person as much as being right, winning, and self-preserving. So a verbal beating-down seems appropriate. Yelling loudly seems appropriate; whatever it takes to win. But when you win this way, you really lose. You lose what at one time was the most important thing in your life, and that is the love relationship you had with your spouse. Remember when you were friends and loved being together? That is now gone, because your fighting to win at all costs has destroyed it. As you enter into conflict, you have to remember that you don't want the team to break up. You are better together than apart.

Part Five

Sleeping Together

Chapter 12

Sex in Today's Culture

There is nothing we can discuss about marriage that is more explosive than the subject of sleeping together or, more accurately, sex. This is the sex sextion … err … section.

Sex in marriage is a huge component of togetherness. If husband and wife aren't together in this area, then the whole marriage is off-kilter. Once in a while, we will run across a sexless marriage, and every time it is a weak marriage heading for divorce or, at the very least, loneliness, pornography issues, masturbation, and adultery. Sex isn't everything, but it affects every part of our relationship. That's how God designed it. Sex was meant to bring intimacy in a way nothing else can between a husband and wife. Sex enriches every part of marriage. That's why it's meant to be shared between married couples only. Sex outside of marriage is immature sex, which falls short of its divine purpose of each of us elevating our spouses above all others by the giving of our bodies to them and them alone. In turn, God is glorified through this powerful act of sexual love.

We always encourage couples to live by this one rule on sex: "One hundred percent of my sexuality is for my spouse." This takes the guesswork out it. For a married couple, flirting at the office, fantasizing over pictures on one of your screens, reading overly sexualized romance novels, and any other type of sexual activity, no matter how small or insignificant it seems, is to be avoided and your sex saved for each other and only each other. We are not to share our sexuality with anyone else. The 100 percent rule keeps us within safe boundaries and, more importantly, keeps us thinking only about each other.

The Apostle Paul wrote about this in 1 Corinthians 7:3–5 (NIV). He wrote, "The husband should fulfill his marital duty to his wife, and likewise the wife to the husband; The wife does not have authority over her own body but yields it to her husband. In the same way, the husband does not have authority over his own body but yields it to his wife; Do not deprive each other except perhaps by mutual consent and for a time, so that you may devote yourselves to prayer. Then come together again so Satan will not tempt you because of your lack of self-control."

Paul gives us a key to sexual fulfillment—the mutual submission of our bodies to each other to satisfy the sexual needs and desires of each of us. This is an easy one for me to sign up for! My body and its sexual abilities is for my wife to enjoy for her pleasure—and hers mine. What a deal! Thank you, God. The only time sexual restraint is encouraged is during times of fasting, prayer, and seeking God. But even then it's only for a short time frame, and then it's back at it. Notice how Paul connects sexual frequency with self-control? Lots of good sex results in limited opportunity or even desire for sex outside of your marriage. When sex isn't frequent, then trouble begins. The "Sleeping Together" section is designed to help you understand God's design for sex. It's practical and will hopefully inspire you to enjoy sex a lot more. It's been over thirty years for my wife and I enjoying one another and one another only. And it's amazing how sex still excites us; it gets better and keeps us safe in each other's arms. Once again, thank you, God, for sex! You knew what you were doing.

Let's start our discussion by looking at the cultural worldview of sex. You don't have to look very hard to find it. Our computers, phones, televisions, and movie screens show us. The Internet explains it. Our friends brag ... err ... talk about it.

First, society's perspective of sex is based on the humanistic philosophy that all of life is limited to what human beings make of it. In other words, it is man's ability to reason and figure out the mysteries of existence, through scientific discoveries and through utilizing our own intelligence and human reasoning, that determines how we live our lives. Humanism is life without any input from a spiritual source. That train of thought leads to the belief that humans consist of only body and soul. Man has no spirit; we are spiritless. So when it comes to our sexual nature, sex is seen simply as a physical activity to be enjoyed by our bodies. There is nothing spiritual about the sexual experience between people. In fact, with technological advances, sex doesn't need to be between people anymore. There is now virtual-reality porn, during which people wear a headset while watching a virtual-reality porn video. This is described as being a "scary real" experience by the author of an online article titled "VR Porn Is Here and It's Scary How Realistic It Is." [1] Another tech development is the creation of "sexbots," which are robots designed to engage in sexual activities with humans. [2] Not to be too graphic here, but technology is now creating gels and devices that allow couples to stimulate each other without being in the same room. [3] Yes, it's getting freaky out there.

A couple of years ago, I began hearing about what is currently known as the "hookup culture." Hookup culture is the descriptive label given to the sexual environment that exists on college campuses, bars, and clubs, where mostly young people hang out, meet someone, and "hook up." Hooking up is defined as participating in sexual acts with someone you just met and have no attachment to. In her book, *Unhooked: How Young Women Pursue Sex, Delay Love and Lose at Both*, author Laura Sessions Stepp describes what hookup culture,—or as she describes it, "unhooked culture"—looks like on college campuses.

"Young people have virtually abandoned dating and replaced it with group get-togethers and sexual behaviors that are detached from love or commitment—and sometimes even from liking."

"Relationships have been replaced by the casual sexual encounters known as hookups. Love, while desired by some, is being put on hold or seen as impossible; sex is becoming the primary currency of social interaction."

"Hooking up's defining characteristic is the ability to unhook from a partner at any time, just as they might get rid of an old song on their iPod or an out-of-date "away" message on their computer. Maybe they tire of their partner, or they find someone who is "hotter" or for some other reason more to their liking. Maybe they get burned badly in a relationship or find themselves swamped with term papers and final exams. The freedom to unhook from someone—ostensibly without repercussions—gives them maximum flexibility. Although I use both phrases, this is not a *hookup* culture so much as an *unhooked* culture. It is a way of thinking about relationships, period."[4]

The key thought in her analysis is what Ms. Stepp describes as "the ability to unhook from a partner at any time." This philosophical view of sex is the total opposite and diametrically opposed to God's design for sex. Sex is what "hooks" a husband and wife together. You can't unhook what God uses to hook.

Paul describes this in 1 Corinthians 6:13-20 (NIV). "You say "Food for the stomach and the stomach for food, and God will destroy them both." The body, however, is not meant for sexual immorality but for the Lord, and the Lord for the body. By his power God raised the Lord from the dead, and he will raise us also. Do you not know that your bodies are members of Christ himself? Shall I take the members of Christ and unite them with a prostitute? Never! Do you not know that he who unites himself with a prostitute is one with her in body? For it is said, "The two will become one flesh." But whoever is united with the Lord is one with him in spirit. Flee from sexual immorality. All other sins a person commits are outside the body, but whoever sins sexually, sins against their own body. Do you not know that your bodies are temples of the Holy Spirit, who is in you, whom you have received from God? You are not your own; you were bought at a price. Therefore honor God with your bodies."

Sexual sin is any sexual activity outside of marriage. I'm not including holding hands and a goodnight kiss between a couple in love who are moving their relationship toward marriage. Those are signs of affection, and if kept innocent, they stay that way. But when we move into areas of intense sexual activity that lead down the path to sexual intercourse, that is where boundary lines are crossed and physical shows of affection turn into sin. Paul is saying that sexual sin is different than any other kind of sin. It involves not just our bodies but our souls (minds, wills and emotions). That's why sexual sin causes so much emotional pain. Let me put it this way. Sex is in fact a *spiritual and emotional* hookup, not just a physical one. Ms. Stepp makes the connection in her book.

"Says Susan Nolen-Hoeksema, a University of Michigan psychologist who researches depression, 'Something about dating behavior and dating relationships can be toxic to girls' health.' Significantly, the shorter the relationship, the more likely depression will show up. Most hookups are nothing if not brief. This means that girls who hook up serially have to work very hard—harder than they may know or admit—to squash or deny natural feelings of connection, making themselves even more vulnerable to depression."5

Did you catch that? To *quash or deny natural feelings of connection.* Quashing or denying those natural God-designed feelings leaves a woman feeling empty. God designed sex to be a connection between a husband and wife. When they participate in sex outside of marriage, it becomes twisted. It's like coloring outside the lines. Things are sexually no longer in order, according to God's will and purpose. The result is hurt, depression, a feeling of being used and unvalued, even abused. And the biggest reality check—unplanned pregnancies compound the problem by obliging a woman to deal with the huge decisions a pregnancy presents.

Men have issues also. Michael Kimmel is a professor of sociology and a scholar in the field of gender studies at State University of New York. In his book titled, *Guyland: The Perilous World Where Boys Become Men*," he writes about hookup culture from a young man's perspective.

"Sex in Guyland is just that—guys' sex. Women are welcome to act upon their sexual desires, but guys run the scene. Women who decide not to join the party can look forward to going to sleep early and alone tonight—and every night. And women who do join the party run the risk of encountering the same old double standard that no amount of feminist progress seems able to eradicate fully. Though women may accommodate themselves to men's desires—indeed, some feel they have to accommodate themselves to them—the men's rules rule. What this means is that many young women are biding their time, waiting for the guys to grow up and start acting like men."6

What Dr. Kimmel is addressing is a huge problem for women today. Young men display the maturity level of junior-high boys. A man who is mature controls his sexual impulses and saves them for marriage. An immature man's sexuality is unrestrained and used against women to satisfy his urges. Unfortunately, many women have lowered the standard of their expectations on how men should act and willingly participate in hooking up with immature, noncommittal guys.

Second, society promotes participation in reckless sexuality without people having thought through the potential consequences. Society says, "Act on impulse." "Sex is an exciting adventure waiting to be taken." "There are no consequences for you and your sexual behavior; that only happens to other people." As a result of this mind-set, society encourages men to have copious amounts of sex with many different partners. As already mentioned, this results in young men delaying maturity and preparation for marriage. What is the motivation for marriage if he can have sex without the commitment? If he can move on when he tires of his current sex partner? For men, God designed sex as the big payoff for committing to marriage and fulfilling their God-given responsibility as husbands who love, care, and provide for their wives.

In today's culture the average age of a man losing his virginity is sixteen, and for women it's seventeen.[7] Most people aren't married yet at that young age. Further studies show that a large percentage of American teenagers and college students are exceedingly sexually active.

I've seen research on the number of sex partners men and women have in their lifetimes, and men always average more partners than do women. (Then I read a survey that showed men also lie more when answering this question, so we don't really know if that's true.) But in today's culture, women seem to be as sexually carefree and emotionally detached as men. It's like wearing a badge of honor. Hollywood culture sends the message that sex, either heterosexual or homosexual, is the ultimate experience in life, and if you are not having sex constantly, then you are missing out and something is wrong with you.

Third, society takes no stand on saving sexuality exclusively for marriage. In fact, it promotes just the opposite. Society says that you should have sex before marriage to make sure are you compatible sexually. Or they say that if you are already married you should have sex outside of your marriage to add some spice to your life. This is the purpose for a website that arranges affairs for married people. Established in 2001, www.ashleymadison.com had over twenty-two million users from thirty countries. Its slogan is, "Life is short; have an affair." Recently this website company made headline news as hackers stole the email addresses of the men and woman who'd registered with the company and paid the monthly fee for access to willing adultery partners. Some well-known people were among them. According to the reports, marriages were ruined, jobs were lost, pastors resigned from their pulpits, and worse, at least four men, including a pastor, took their own lives rather than face their wives.[8] While ashleymadison.com celebrates and profits from adultery, families suffer.

Dr. Larry Crabb writes about the damage of what he calls *fun* sex—that is, sex outside of marriage, which people participate in for fun. Dr. Crabb says, "sex that for a moment helps a woman feel desirable, feminine, wanted, secure; sex that enables a man to feel attractive, adequate, manly, significant. But Satan cannot offer meaningful relationship built on loving commitment to one another. Fun sex is a charade. It satisfies the body but leaves the real person empty and despairing. It offers pleasure for the body without meaning for the person."[9]

It's what "fun sex" leaves out that brings the pain. Sex was meant for the body *with* emotional and spiritual meaning for the married couple who enjoys it. Sex is more than physical. Paul teaches us that we are "triune" beings, consisting of body, soul (mind, will, emotions), and spirit.

In 1 Thessalonians 5:23 (NIV), Paul writes, "May God himself, the God of peace sanctify through and through. May your whole spirit, soul and body be kept blameless at the coming of our Lord Jesus Christ."

There is a spiritual component to sex that some in society are unaware of. As long as sex is just physical, then the act will be fun and pleasurable, but the spiritual and emotional consequences will leave deep wounds.

"God's will is for you to be holy, so stay away from all sexual sin. Then each of you will control his own body and live in holiness and honor—not in lustful passion like the pagans who do not know God and his ways. Never harm or cheat a fellow believer in this matter by violating his wife, for the Lord avenges all such sins, as we have solemnly warned you before. God has called us to live holy lives, not impure lives. Therefore, anyone who refuses to live by these rules is not disobeying human teaching but is rejecting God, who gives his Holy Spirit to you" (1 Thessalonians 4:3–8 NLT).

For followers of Christ, sexual morality is a huge battle when faced with society's message. In our flesh we desire to have a lot of sex with a lot of people. But the fact remains that sex outside of marriage is damaging. Sexual immorality is *sin*, according to Scripture. It's breaking God's law and defying his purpose for our sexuality. And when we break it, sin brings its consequences with it. The consequences include the feelings we've described in this chapter upon the soul. Guilt, shame, and humiliation are a few by-products of sex outside of marriage. Sex outside of marriage is fun for a pleasurable moment. But it's not so fun once the moment has passed and the consequences come.

Thank God for his grace, mercy, and forgiveness through Jesus. Jesus's work on the cross took all of our guilt, shame, and humiliation upon him, so our sexuality can be free, healed, and whole again within the bonds of marriage! But only through accepting him as our Savior, and then obeying his laws found in Scripture, will we experience true healing and be able to move forward in life. Yes, sexuality can be broken through our sinful behaviors, but through Christ and his mercy, it can be healed through grace!

Chapter 13

Sex in God's Eyes

We've seen how society views sexuality. Let's now look at God's view of sex.

I really love classic cars, especially American muscle cars. I've see some beautiful classics over the years—Chevy Corvettes, Malibu's, Camaro's, Ford Mustangs, Pontiac GTO's and Dodge Chargers. I've touched them, sat in them, and even driven one. But never have I owned one. I'm still holding out hope! In this chapter, let's not just look at sex, but let's own our sexuality by looking at it from God's point of view. This will give us a whole different perspective.

First, God created our bodies for sex. Back to Genesis 1:27: "So God created mankind in his own image, in the image of God he created them; *male* and *female* he created them" (italic emphasis mine). It's obvious when looking at the human body that certain male and female body parts were meant to ... um ... *coexist* with each other. God created sex as a natural part of our human bodily functions.

Second, sex is what allows us to fulfill the "be fruitful and multiply" commandment in Genesis 1:28. There were no other options that Adam and Eve could come up with to have some kids! They could have planted some seeds in the ground and watered them, but no kids would sprout up. There were no kids to adopt, even if they'd wanted to. Have you ever wondered what that first sexual experience for Adam and Eve was like? I know, that's weird. But really, be honest. You know you have. Did God have the birds-and-bees chat with them? Or did he leave it to them to figure it out? Did nature truly take its course? Well, obviously it did. I wonder what Adam said after God gave the be-fruitful-and-multiply commandment? "Well, Eve. First of all, nice to meet you. You have nice pair of … err … eyes. Oh, and happy wedding to you. Whew, this has all happened so fast. I mean, don't be offended, but I just met you, and now we're married. I'm just not sure yet what it all means. Um, can I ask you a question? Do you have any idea what God meant when he told us to multiply? O-o-o-oh, make more of us. I see. *Hmm.* I was made out of mud, and you were made out of me. Not sure how to make another one of us. Do you have any ideas? Well, yes, I did notice that you and I are different down there. Is that supposed to mean something? *Whoa*, never thought of that. Yeah, that might just work. Are you sure you want to try that? Seems a little awkward, but if you're willing to give it a go, let's see what happens." A little while later: "Well, that seemed to work just fine. Can we do that again?"

God literally mandated that married couples have sex and create children. I call it God's greatest trick. He made the baby-making process really fun so we'd want to make them, and he made babies really cute so we'd want to have them. No fair.

Third, sex was viewed by God (and eventually Adam and Eve) as *very* good. "And God looked over all he had made, and he saw that it was very good" (Genesis 1:31). So sex is not to be viewed by Christians as evil, dirty, perverted, or as a procreation duty to be performed out of obligation. He wants married couples to enjoy it!

Fourth, husbands and wives glorify God in their shared sexuality. God created sex. God blessed sex in marriage. God wants you to have it. God wants you to enjoy it. And think about this: God is glorified when we participate in it. That's right! We glorify God when enjoying sex as married couples. He is not embarrassed by it. He isn't disgusted by it. He doesn't even look away when we have it (think about that next time), but he is glorified in the act of husband and wife sharing the joys of what he created.

Fifth, sex is relational, meaning only to be shared between a husband and wife. Adam was alone, and God said it wasn't good. So God brought Adam a beautiful woman. Together they shared the wonderful sexual experience that resulted in children but also a relational closeness that was between them and them alone. Genesis 2:24–25 (NIV) describes this: "That is why man leaves his father and mother and is united to his wife, and they become one flesh. Adam and his wife were both naked, and *they felt no shame*" (italics mine).

Timothy Keller writes in his book, *The Meaning of Marriage*, "Indeed, sex is perhaps the most powerful God-created way to help you give your entire self to another human being. Sex is God's appointed way for two people to reciprocally say to one another, "I belong completely, permanently, and exclusively to you."[1] There is nothing more relational and meaningful then an uninhibited and free sexual relationship in marriage.

Last, sex is to be enjoyed. You might be surprised to know that there are some Christian couples that struggle in the area of enjoying sex. Maybe you are one of those. There are many reasons for this. One spouse might have been a victim of sexual abuse and has a tough time overcoming the feelings of being taken advantage of. Some spouses were raised in very strict, unhealthy religious upbringings and were never taught that sex was to be enjoyed, but instead it was always reinforced that sex was sinful, so they had to be careful. Some have never acquired the skills necessary to be good lovers and bring pleasure to their spouses in that way. For others there are medical reasons that their bodies aren't able to function properly sexually. I encourage you to seek medical help if you suffer from this condition. But when you read the Bible, you see numerous times that romance and sex are to be enjoyed. I would encourage you to read the most romantic and erotic book in the Bible, The Song of Solomon. The sensual metaphors, romantic language, and vivid descriptions of sexual acts make interesting and enjoyable reading. This Biblical telling of romantic love in the Song of Solomon describes all kinds of sexually fun stuff between a husband and wife. From sex in the bedroom to sex outside under a tree. From standard intercourse to oral sex. Yes, the Bible goes there. And it's all good. Hey, guys, you have God's blessing to enjoy sex with each other!

Let me show you how that can happen.

Chapter 14

Men—What Your Wife Wants

Men, to have a positive, fulfilling and meaningful sex life, you need to know what women want when it comes to sex. I want to let you know right from start that I had help on this section. I asked my wife. "Autumn, I need to ask you something. What is it that women want when it comes to sex with their husbands?"

"You're not going to like my answers," she replied.

"Oh. Can you tell me anyway, because after thirty-plus years of marriage, I probably need to know this stuff—even if it's just for your sake." We had a good laugh, but the answers she gave me as we started our discussion did make me realize how often I'd missed giving her the best experience I could have. This next statement might fall into the category of "over-sharing," but after thirty years of marriage we marvel at times how our sex life keeps getting better.

Men, here you go. And ladies, you are next. You get the next chapter.

What Women Want: Affection

Women want to feel what the dictionary defines as "a gentle feeling of fondness or liking." That's the definition of affection.

Your wife wants to know that you *like* her. She knows you love her, but do you *like* her? She wants you to want to spend time with her, as you do with your man buddies. Many husbands blow it by treating their man buddies better than they do their wives. To those guys, their wives aren't friends as much as they are cooks, maids, and sex partners. Husbands express this when they aren't interested in doing anything together, like when date nights are nonexistent, or life at home is more like two roommates sharing a house than a husband and a wife sharing a life. A wife also feels a lack of affection when her husband gets more excited when his man buddy drives up on his Harley than he does when she walks through the front door after a long day at the office, when they haven't seen each other for hours.

Affection is like a warm summer breeze you feel while sitting under a shade tree. It just feels good. It feels right. Affection is spending quality time over coffee and talking about life. Affection is telling her how beautiful she is and how much you like being with her. Affection is buying a small gift that is more thoughtful then expensive. Affection is letting her know that she is more valuable than any other person in the world to you. And affection begins the process of a woman opening herself up, both body and soul, to her man and desiring him in her bed that night.

What Women Want: Intimate Conversation

We've already spent three chapters on talking together, but it is worth going down one more level here. Intimate conversation is a very important part of a thriving sex life for married couples. This is where some husbands fall short. That's because intimate conversation means taking your talking to a whole 'nother level, where you share intimate thoughts or things about yourself. *How are you feeling right now about life? What are your current dreams? What is God speaking to you during this season? What are you afraid of? What are you concerned about?* Most men don't like going there. It's hard. It's humbling. It's exactly what your wife wants to hear from you. Women communicate on a different wavelength. Men love surface. Women love depth.

When I would go ocean fishing, there would be two of us in a boat, with four fishing poles. The fishing poles would be let down to different levels in the water. A couple of fishing poles were set shallow, where we hoped to catch the fish swimming closer to the surface. The other two poles would be let down deeper into the water. If we were fishing for halibut, we would let the lines drop all the way to the bottom of the ocean, up to three hundred feet down. Surface versus deep. I'm surfacey. That is not a real word, but it sounds cool and makes the point. I prefer light and humorous conversation when at home, because my day is oftentimes spent dealing with deep, heavy, and emotional things that people in our church are experiencing. Autumn prefers de-e-e-e-e-p. It's hard for me to get there, but I have learned that when I reach down deep, open my heart to her, and have intimate conversations with Autumn, I feel closer to her. Her feedback is valuable to me. I feel heard. I feel understood. Most of all, I can tell that she feels loved and closer to me when I let my "man guard" down and welcome her in. And I will tell you that many times after a conversation like that, *ooh la* happens. And it's at a level deeper than physical. It's emotional. It's powerful. It's halibut.

What Women Want: Nonsexual Touch

Nonsexual touch is another thing a woman wants. I didn't know there was such a thing. Go figure. The reason I held Autumn's hand was to get to the next step. But I learned that's not how it works in woman's world. In woman's world, holding hands has nothing to do with sex later but feeling valued and cherished now. Nonsexual touch has everything to do with your wife feeling loved without sex being involved. Men, read that last sentence *s l o w l y*, because I'm sure you didn't get it. Yes, there is a touch that simply says, "I love you. I love being with you right now. I'm not even thinking about sex at this minute. That last thing about not thinking about sex was a lie, but I really do love you and love being with you." That's what nonsexual touch is. Holding her hand while walking together. Squeezing her shoulders when you pass behind her. Giving her a foot massage while watching TV together. Brushing her cheek when you say good morning as you first see her when waking up. A long, full-body hug when you come home from work. (I hope you husbands are writing this down, because I am definitely helping you here.) Nonsexual touch is a valid expression of affection and opens the door to her heart and her body to receive more explicit touches during sex. Take it from a former sexual toucher: this way is the better way.

What Women Want: A Husband Who Knows What He Is Doing

A man's body can be ready for sexual intercourse in fourteen seconds. Put your stop watches away; just trust me on this. I don't know why God made us this way. It's a little embarrassing, to be honest. Have you ever told your wife that you just wanted to cuddle? Before you know it … "I thought you said you just wanted to cuddle!"

"Sorry—I can't help it!"

When everything is working right, as men, we are ready to go. Women, on the other hand, need time for their bodies to warm up. Many husbands move too fast, and because their wives' bodies aren't ready, the whole experience is unpleasant or at least unfulfilling. Good sex takes good timing. Husbands, it's always good to go slow. As it's been said, slow and steady wins the race. It's good to learn how to please your wife in ways other than intercourse. A sensitive husband will learn about his wife's sexual needs and desires and do his best to bring pleasure to her before experiencing pleasure himself. In this way you are serving your wife and placing her needs above your own. Here is how it works. When you put her sexual needs *above your own,* the result will be that your personal sexual needs will be more than met, because in return for your meeting hers, she'll want to meet yours. The biblical principle of "it's more blessed to give then to receive" applies to every area of life, including our sex lives. I encourage men to always wait until their wives *let them know* that they are ready for the "big event." When you practice patience and allow nature to take its course, the payoff will be better than you imagine.

Sex takes skill. The more a man learns and practices (with his wife, of course), the better a lover he will be. And hey, guys, it's not a sinful thing to read up on how to be to a better lover. There are Christian resources for couples that address these areas. I would encourage every couple to read one or all:

The Act of Marriage, by Tim and Beverly LaHaye
His Needs, Her Needs, by Willard Harley
Sheet Music, by Dr. Kevin Leman
Intended for Pleasure, by Ed Wheat
A Celebration of Sex, by Dr. Douglas E. Rosenau

Women love sex as much as men do. Don't be fooled into thinking otherwise. The better you get at it, the more she'll want it. And that is what every man wants!

Chapter 15

Women—What Your Husband Wants

Again, I want to give credit to my wife, Autumn, for sharing her insights and notes from her teaching on this topic. So the following principles are being written by me, but they have been influenced by her insights and wisdom from a woman's perspective.

Sexual intimacy was created by God for marriage. It is a beautiful experience. Sex can take both husbands and wives to physical heights of pleasure that are indescribable.

Sexual intimacy is holy. Sex in marriage is a renewal and a celebration of a couple's covenant to each other. Sex is the seal of the covenant of marriage. God created sex for us to enjoy. Proverbs 5:18–19 says, "Let your fountain be blessed, and rejoice with the wife of your youth. As a loving deer and a graceful doe, let her breasts satisfy you at all times; and always be enraptured with her love" (NKJV). This is very romantic metaphoric language that is basically telling husbands to enjoy sex with their wives and to be satisfied with their sexuality and theirs alone. It also advises couples to always make themselves available to each other for sexual fulfillment.

Secrets to a Woman's Sexual Fulfillment

Before we get to the topic of what your husband wants in sex, let's answer some questions.

What are you thinking about sex? For both men and women, the biggest sex organ is the brain. Our thought life is where sexual activity begins. For men, thoughts quickly trigger a physical response and physical desire for sex. Women can also experience this, but for the most part a women's thoughts trigger an emotional desire for sex. Uncontrolled emotional desires for sex can result in sinful sexual fantasies. It's important for women to guard their minds from these. The fantasies I'm referring to are sexual desires for men other than your husband. A women's sexual fantasies can be triggered by romance novels with explicit sexual content in them. The same goes for movies or television shows. The result of uncontrolled sexual fantasy will be discontent with your husband's sexual prowess when in your mind you aren't thinking in reality. You will be setting your husband up for failure. You have to pattern your sexual life around your husband being the only man who will arouse you. Unrestrained sexual daydreaming can have you in the arms of another man and damaging your marriage. Paul encourages the Church in 2 Corinthians 10:5 to "take captive every thought and make it obedient to Christ." The word *captive* conjures up images of someone being bound hand and foot and carried away against her will. Your mind will *want* to dwell on sexual fantasy, to bind your sexuality hand and foot and carry you away to a world of sexual destruction. So *you* have to do the binding. Bind those thoughts and carry them away. Don't let your mind get wrapped up in *Fifty Shades of Grey* (a graphic erotic sex novel for women which sold over a hundred million copies in 2011).

The Bible is a weapon that defeats our enemies when it's used in spiritual battle. The battle of the mind is a struggle we all face. Quoting scripture is the most effective way to withstand the onslaught. It's the weapon Jesus used himself in Matthew 4:1–11. When Satan tempted Jesus in his thoughts by offering him food when he was fasting, to test his obedience to God, Jesus responded the same way each time. He said, "It is written …" and then quoted the verses from the book of Deuteronomy. He effectively took every thought captive by binding the evil thoughts of temptation with the Word of God. Jesus, in his humanness, was able to resist temptation. Using the same strategy, you can resist temptation as well. When your mind is faced with tempting thoughts of sexual fantasy, quote the Word of God. Here is a list of great verses to use in your arsenal. Personalize them. Insert your name in them. There is power in God's living Word. Psalm 119:9, 11; 1 Corinthians 6:18–20; 1 Thessalonians 4:3–7; Galatians 5:16, 17, 22; Philippians 4:8. Read these verses out loud. Something strengthens our will when we quote the Bible out loud. Our actions tend to follow our words. Use the power of confession to bring change to your thought patterns.

What are you thinking about yourself? Many of you struggle with self-esteem, and that can directly affect your experience in the bedroom. If you measure your self-worth according to society's standards of beauty, you will fall short—unless, of course, you can afford to hire a hair stylist, makeup artist, personal trainer, personal chef, and a photographer/editor who is an expert at photo-shopping all your selfies. You must find self-esteem somewhere else, or more exactly, in some*one* else—and it's not your husband. Even your husband can't provide that for you. Your self-esteem must be found in Jesus Christ. Only Jesus can fill the holes in your heart. Only he can complete the puzzle that makes up your life. As a wife, you may desire more attention and more affection from your husband. Let me tell you straight up; he can't meet all of those desires. He is human, and trust me, he is lacking.

By looking to Jesus every day and finding your self-worth in his perfect love, perfect acceptance, and perfect will for you, you will find all the self-esteem you need. Jesus must fulfill you first. If you look to your husband to complete you, he will fail, and you will remain unfulfilled and suffering. You husband can't be God to you. He can't fill your heart or feed your spirit. Fill your heart with God's presence through daily times of prayer and worship. Feed your spirit on his Word by reading the Bible each day. I know it sounds weird, but having a close relationship with Jesus and finding yourself in him and his perfect love will enhance your sexual intimacy with your husband. This results when you are feeling good about yourself and exhibiting a confidence that you've found in Jesus. When you approach sex from an attitude of confidence instead of from a lack of self-assuredness, it's better for both you and your husband. You will both experience a greater freedom in bed. You will want to *give* your husband more of yourself than you *receive* from him. You will initiate sex more often, and that's a good thing. You will be open to trying new sexual adventures, and that's a good thing. Self-confidence is a key ingredient to a full, fun, and satisfying sex life.

What are you thinking about your husband? I've addressed the subject of the danger of having sexual fantasies that don't include your husband. But what if they do include your husband? Go for it! Instead of thinking all the time about what he's lacking, or what he needs to change, think instead about the good in him. Think about the sweet things he has said to you. Think about how hard he works to provide a life for you. Think about what you appreciate about him. And yes, if you like how he looks naked, then think about that. Think about former sexual experiences together that shot you to the moon and back. Thinking about your husband in a sexual way is appropriate and beneficial. Sexual thoughts produce hormones in your body that bring joy and create desire. As long as your husband is the subject of your thoughts, then fantasize away!

What are you saying? In the arena of sexual intimacy, words have the power to create a positive, sexually charged atmosphere filled with energy and passion, or the power to create the opposite effect. If a wife speaks to her husband in a disrespectful manner or is demanding or angry, he won't want to be with her sexually. You read that correctly. As much as men crave sex, they will pass on having sex with a wife who disrespects them. Most men respond to encouraging words and shut down at discouraging words. The quality of a married couple's sex life is directly influenced by the quality of the words spoken between them.

What are you doing? The cliché "actions speak louder than words" has been around for so long because it's true. Actions are also a huge part of the equation. Let's look at a few things you can do to enhance your sex life.

What Men Want: To Be the Object of Your Flirtation

A wife should practice discretion in your relationships with men other than your husband. Any type of flirtation is off-limits. When you flirt, you are trying to attract someone who is not your husband. You do this by being overly friendly and spending too much time giving focused attention. Smiling playfully, inappropriate touches, or double-entendre joking sends the message that you would like a deeper relationship with each other than is appropriate. Past romantic relationships should also be carefully guarded. No contact ever is the safest way, but at the least set boundaries of appropriateness if there is need for communication.

What Men Want: To Not Be Deprived

A wife should never withhold sex to punish your husband. Believe it or not, that is a sin against your husband (and vice versa. This goes both ways.). 1 Corinthians 7:4–5 says, "The wife gives authority over her body to her husband, and the husband gives authority over his body to his wife. Do not deprive each other of sexual relations" (NLT). Withholding sex because you are angry and want revenge will cause him to be tempted to get his sex somewhere else. Sex during times of relational tension can actually help the restoration process, because that communicates that you are still on the same team and working together to find solutions. It's hard to have sex and remain enemies.

What Men Want: For You to Be the Responder.

Yes, there are times when he will pursue you sexually and you just aren't up for it. That is totally okay. Learn to communicate honestly with him when that occurs. But for the most part, when you are a responder to his sexual advances, he will be his most passionate, because he senses that you desire him physically. And that pays off for you in the end.

What Men Want: For You to Be the Initiator.

If you really want to freak him out, be an aggressive initiator of sex. He won't know what to do and might even run out of the room yelling, "Who are you and what have you done with my wife!" It really does make sex fun when a husband and wife take turns initiating sex. Men and woman both can get turned on physically on different days at different times, and both should feel that they can initiate and not be turned down or rejected.

What Men Want: Moments of Spontaneity

Take advantage of the moment! Trust me, as parents of four children, we have found those moments few and far between. Lunch-hour quickies, closet sex, quiet sex, car-in-the-garage sex, interrupted-by-the-door-knock ("Dad, can I come in and ask you a question?") sex—we've done it all. And to be honest, those are some of our favorite memories as we look back and laugh. If you are feeling it, make it happen.

What Men Want: Buy Some Stuff

Wives, make some purchases. Investing money in your sex life is a worthy place to spend some cash. Fragrances, special bedsheets, lighting, candles, and lingerie are among items that enhance our sexual experiences.

What Men Want: To Both Be Learners.

There is so much more to our bodies than we realize in the area of sexuality. There is an art to sex. There is skill required to bring a full sexual experience to your spouse. The more you know, the better sex partner you'll become. In the last chapter, I list five books for men that would be a great help for you in this area.

There are women who struggle with releasing their sexuality for themselves or their husbands to enjoy due to horrific sexually abusive actions by men. Are you one of these women? Sexual sin met you early; it hurt you and made you feel guilty or ashamed. I want you to know that there is hope for you. In Christ, you can experience complete freedom from that bondage. Your sexuality can be restored and fulfilled in marriage. It's not easy. The memories don't leave. But the pain and sorrow can be overcome, with the love of your heavenly Father and at the hands and body of a loving husband. We would encourage you, if needed, to find specialized counseling or a support system of women who can help you if you are struggling with this. God will make you whole!

What Sex Means to Men

Sex for a man means fulfillment of a physical need. Men's bodies produce large levels of testosterone. Testosterone is a sex hormone that is found in both men and women, but it occurs in much larger amounts in men. This chemical in men produces sperm and triggers the sex drive. So, a man has this chemical in his body that creates his desire to have a physical-sexual release of the sperm his body has created. I know this doesn't sound romantic at all. But facts are facts, and a man needs a sexual physical release at certain times. His body demands it. You've heard of wet dreams. When a young man hits puberty, the testosterone kicks in, and he will ejaculate in his sleep. It's not perverse, it's not creepy; it's his body's natural way of "taking care of business." Likewise, as a married man, your husband will have days when his body craves and needs a sexual release. That's why regular sex with your husband is a good idea, because that release is going to happen with or without you. Withholding sex from your husband is never a good idea. That will open the door to him seeking sex outside of your marriage, whether via the Internet or with someone other than you. That sexual release that he shares with you creates a level of masculine satisfaction and physical fulfillment, which relaxes him, creates a more stable emotional environment for him, and releases the inner caveman that wants to show his woman what he's made of. God created men to conquer. Letting him catch and conquer you sexually is very meaningful to him. And you will receive the benefit of having a sexually satisfied husband.

Sex reinforces his manhood and builds self-confidence in all areas of his life. A confident man is a successful man. You can't underestimate the importance of this dynamic. Your husband needs to know that he is pleasing his wife. Let yourself go during sex. Give verbal responses and let him know you like what he's doing. By communicating your positive experience during sex, you will build up his confidence, and he'll respond by becoming *more* of a man during sex. He'll become more adventuresome, more aggressive (in a good way, not a hurtful way), and more creative. A wise woman lets her husband know he is a good lover.

Sex can also elevate his spirit during a discouraging time. If he has lost his job, didn't get the promotion, or has had his ego deflated by a hard meeting with the boss, a good sexual experience with you can lift him up. Initiating sex during times of a man's discouragement will remind him that he is loved by you no matter what life's circumstances. He'll be encouraged, because you still see him as a man, a sexual hunk of love that is desirable to you even on a bad day. Sex communicates to him your confidence in him in terms that he understands. He is thinking, "I'm a loser. I'm not a good husband, not a good father; I'm a failure," but when you come on to him like he's the sex god that you've been desiring all day, he'll get the idea that you still believe in him. I have personally been through extremely discouraging times, including losses of jobs, ministry challenges, and financial hardship. I can attest to the fact that during these low times Autumn gave me very high times sexually and helped me rebound back to normal. I knew she wasn't giving up on me but still believed in me and desired me. Sex can be an emotional healer for your husband.

Sex enhances his love for you. I mentioned the physical need aspect of sex for a man, but let me also say that men have emotional needs as well. Men are more than sex machines! Sex for a man is also a love enhancer. Because sex is very important to his overall well-being as a man, having consistent, creative, engaging sexual experiences with you will make him love you more. When you buy something at Victoria's Secret and wear it with confidence, his love for you will be enhanced. When you speak to him with a loving tone of voice and with encouraging words, his love for you will be enhanced. When you receive his compliments with visible gratitude and thankfulness, his love for you will be enhanced. When you respond to his sexual advances with authentic desire, his love for you will be enhanced. When he knows that every part of your body is available to him and you are holding nothing back, his love for you will be enhanced. Sex reaches his emotions, not just his body.

Sex reduces friction and brings peace. During times of tension in your relationship, sometimes he doesn't need to have a big talk to relieve it. Sex can do the job just fine. Sex helps him to handle the stress of the kids, his job or finances. Sex isn't what fixes problems. But it does keep his heart open to you and enables him to work with you on making changes and finding solutions.

Sex is more to your husband than a physical thing. It reaches his soul, his inner man, and helps him to become the man that God is calling him to be. You have a big part to play, and I encourage you to play often.

Part Six

Parenting Together

Chapter 16

The Incredibleness of
Parenting Together

One of the great miracles of life is the reproductive ability God gave plants, trees, fish, land animals and, well, us. Genesis 1:11–31 describes Creation and the systems of reproduction. Plants and vegetation were "seed-bearing" and "bear fruit with seed in it, according to their various kinds" (v. 12). Birds, fish and animals were created by God and told to "be fruitful and increase in number and fill the water in the seas, and let the birds increase on the earth" (v. 21–22). It was the same for land animals (v. 24–25), and for humans, but with a huge twist. The twist is that humans are created in the "image of God" (v. 26, 27). This, of course, is what makes humans special. Unlike birds, fish, and land animals, human beings are "like God." That means we actually represent God here on earth, at some level.

The Hebrew meaning of the words *image* and *like us* (or *likeness*) tell us that we reflect God himself and represent him here on earth. Scholars can't agree in which specific areas we are like God. With our finite minds, it might even be a little silly to try to figure it out. But let's give it a go. We have the ability to think, reason, create, and have emotional connections with others, as God does. We carry authority over creation, which seems God-like. I'm sure these characteristics are part of being like God. But there is one thing that strikes me as being the most God-like, and that is the ability to create another human being and, get this—in God's image. Plants, trees, fish, and land animals don't fall into this category. Only us. Humans. We create other God-like humans. It's pretty mind-boggling if you think about it. Through the act of sexual intercourse, we create humans who will represent God here on earth, who will have souls that live forever in eternity.

This is what makes parenting together so important. Our children are representatives of God and they have the potential to make a difference in the world for him. They will add to culture and society in the cities and towns where they will reside. Our children will create, build, develop, manage, and fund our economy. They will become experts in some important area of our society that will make a difference in the lives of people— areas like physics, science, education, sociology, entertainment, design, business, technology, construction, finance, and ministry, to name a few. Our kids will end up somewhere doing something significant for God and humanity. They'll grow up, and if they get married, they'll keep the reproduction cycle moving forward by having their own kids, and *they* will grow up to have their own kids, and … you get the picture. Wow, what an honor! What a responsibility. What a privilege. I love being a parent.

Even secular society sees the need and value of children and healthy parenting. In an article written in the *Orange County Register* titled "Institution of the Family Being Eroded," urban studies expert Joel Kotkin writes about the importance of family and its effect on societies that have devalued familial structures. Kotkin writes,

"For all its limitations, the fundamental values cherished by the religious—notably, family—have never been more important and more in need of moral assistance … Although sensible for many individuals, the decision to detach from familialism augurs poorly for societies, which will be forced to place enormous burdens on a smaller young generation to support an ever-expanding cadre of retirees. It also frames a spiritual crisis in which people no longer look out for their relatives, but only for themselves, inevitably becoming dependent on government to provide the succor that used to come from families."

Families today, notes demographer Wolfgang Lutz, struggle in an environment dominated by adults and their concerns. Many young people grow up without siblings, cousins, and the extended family network so critical to humans for much of our history as a species. Religion, which historically has supported families, has declined in most high-income countries, including, to a lesser extent, the United States, notes the Pew Foundation. Yet celebrating singleness and unmarried families is not progressive in the sense of how it affects children. Broken families are associated with every kind of social dysfunction, from criminality to poverty and mental illness. Human beings, particularly children, Sigmund Freud noted, need a sense that they matter more to their parents than others do; substituting social values for familial ones does not make up for the need of the love that comes naturally to parents. "A love that does not discriminate," he wrote, "seems to me to forfeit a part of its value, by doing an injustice to its object."

Rather than battle over specifics, both social conservatives and pro-family liberals should seek ways to encourage both child-rearing and keeping families intact. Some of these elements are pretty basic: good public education, tax policies that do not penalize married couples, and allowing greater tax deductions for children."[1] God designed the family to care for each other, support one another, and pass down to future generations his blessings. Family matters.

At the time of this writing, Autumn and I have four children and twin grandsons. Our oldest daughter, Rachel, is married to Tim. They have the cute twin boys, Jacob and Caleb. Our second oldest child is Christina. Joshua is next. These three are in their twenties. And finally, we have an eighteen-year-old daughter, Alyssa. Raising these children has been the joy of our lives. It hasn't always been easy, but man, it's been the greatest, most fulfilling thing I've ever done. There have been ups and downs, ins and outs. We've ridden emotional roller coasters. A couple of our kids experienced spiritual crises of faith in their teen years. At times they believed and loved God; at other times they doubted him and wrestled with their spirituality. There have been times of obedience and rebellion. We've walked through boyfriends, girlfriends, and bad breakups. We've cried out to God on our knees for our kids when they were going down destructive paths. We've rejoiced when God answered our prayers and they turned their lives around. As parents we've "been there, done that." I want to share with you some of the things we've learned over the years of raising our children.

My family loves both of the *Father of the Bride* movies, starring Steve Martin and Diane Keaton. My daughters especially like watching the original *Father of the Bride* with me, because I always cry at the ending. They love that. Autumn and I especially love the sequel, *Father of the Bride Part II*, when George and Nina Banks (Steve Martin and Diane Keaton) find out they are pregnant while in their fifties and have to navigate the result of that "little nothing" (a line in the movie describing a passionate moment that took place in the kitchen, resulting in their pregnancy).

One of our favorite scenes takes place in the doctor's office, when the ob/gyn delivers the news that Nina Banks is pregnant. Her husband George's response to the news is one of the funniest comedy scenes ever and a classic. I love watching him overreact to the news. Talking, rambling, saying dumb things to his wife, he stumbles around the doctor's office and finally passes out from the shock. But it's the following scene, the drive home from the doctor's, that we love the most. While Nina is driving their Jeep Cherokee down the street, she is seen smiling, happy, and glowing. She glances out the window on the driver's side of the street and sees a young mom jogging behind a baby stroller with a smile on her face, while George, on the other hand, looks out the passenger side window to see a young boy in an Indian costume running down the street, with his frustrated dad running behind him while dropping a tricycle and stumbling as he tries to keep up. The scene switches back to Nina, now watching another mom holding hands and skipping with her young daughter, both of them laughing. Nina turns and asks George if he's ready to be a parent again. The camera shot goes back to George who, before answering Nina, looks out of the car window to see and hear a young son yelling at his father, very upset that he can't have a hot dog. Meanwhile, the boy is punching the tray of hamburgers and fries that his dad is holding, spilling food all over the front of his dad. With a pained look on his face, George turns to Nina and replies, "I feel super about it. I'm totally up for it."

It doesn't matter whether you feel totally prepared for parenting or you are scared of it; one thing is the same for both circumstances. Once the baby comes, you will be in over your head.

The following chapters skim the surface of parenting and will help you with some general principles that apply to all ages and stages of children. There are many good resources on parenting that go much deeper than I will. This is a book on marriage, not parenting. But I mention parenting because if there is any area of married life that requires a husband and wife to work *together*, it's raising your children. So let's look at "The Main Things," "The Wins," and "The Tools" of parenting together.

Chapter 17

The Main Things

There are three main things that will guarantee your children's success as they grow and mature into adults. Our responsibility as parents is to instill these values into their thoughts, decisions, and behaviors, starting at a very young age. The values are *honesty*, *honor*, and *humility*.

Honesty

Teaching children it's important to always tell the truth is key to their present and future success. Our human nature tempts us to lie when it benefits us. Lying is a self-preservation response to threatening circumstances. Kids lie when they feel that they will get in trouble and receive punishment or are at risk of losing a close friendship or getting a bad grade, or they simply don't want to do their homework. Lying comes naturally to our children. I was a liar as a kid. I didn't start out as a good one. The first lie I remember telling was when I was seven years old. (Remember, I'm telling you about the first lie I can remember. My parents would tell you my lying career started at a much earlier age.) I wasn't just a liar but I was a thief, too. I stole a ring made of candy from the store.

Yep. Just looked around to see if anybody was watching and put it in my pocket. Score! When Mom and I got home, she saw me holding it (admiring my stolen goods like a mafia boss) and asked me where I'd gotten that candy ring. I said, "I just found it in my coat pocket. I think a friend put it in there when I wasn't looking, just being nice." After further interrogation … err … questioning regarding how that candy ring looked just like the ones at the store where we'd just been, I finally broke and confessed. Then I asked for an attorney (not really). I was busted. I couldn't take the pressure. Mom took me back to the store and made me apologize to the store manager (who himself looked like a mafia boss. I still remember his scary black mustache and squinty eyes).

As a teenager, though, I became very good at it. I could lie with the best of them and got away with telling lies about anything I needed to in order to avoid consequences. Now, as an adult, I'm a terrible liar. I guess I'm too holy and spiritual as an adult to lie very well. I can't even lie very well playing the board game Balderdash, which is a game in which you have to lie to win. (Autumn is awesome at that game, which is very concerning to me. But back to the point.) Lying is sinful human nature in its most blatant raw form. My kids started lying pretty early too. The "I didn't do it" response, when in fact they *had* done it, came pretty easy to them. "I didn't eat the cookies; I didn't hit her; I didn't steal his toy; I didn't watch that show; I never looked at that website," and on and on it goes. The result of lying is the breaking of trust in a relationship between parent and child, and that is a high price to pay. So we have to work really hard at establishing a home where the truth is told. There are many things we can do as parents to promote the value of honesty.

First, constantly talk about the value of honesty to your children. From their first lies, reinforce the fact that lying is not acceptable in your home. Let them know that God doesn't want them to lie and that you don't either. When our kids were young we would use positive reinforcement with them, saying things like, "Telling lies isn't like you. You're an honest person and want to tell the truth. So tell Mommy what really happened."

Second, don't lie yourself. We have to model this value to our children. If they catch us in a lie, then in their minds, that gives them license to lie themselves. Whenever Autumn or I made a mistake or broke a promise we'd made to our kids, we never lied to cover it up. It's very meaningful to children when you own up to mistakes and ask them to forgive you. But many times we try to save face by making up an excuse as to why we didn't fulfill a promise, or we lie "a little bit" to avoid humbling ourselves before our kids when they catch us in a mistake. Even worse is if they hear you lying to each other. You can't teach your kids to live one way and then you live another. Hypocrisy in parents creates bitterness and cynicism in children.

Third, make it a rule that in your house truth is rewarded. Our kids knew that if they were caught doing something wrong and they told the truth about it, the punishment would be lessened or even withdrawn. What this does is teach them that it pays dividends to tell the truth. People who lie eventually get caught and pay a steeper price for it. Truth-tellers will experience immediate consequences but overall will usually get off easier. Truth-tellers also live with a clear conscience instead of a guilty conscience, and that is what makes it worth telling the truth.

We could always tell when our kids were living in a lie, because they didn't seem themselves. They weren't as happy; they didn't want to be with the family and would spend time alone in their rooms, or they would just seem to be carrying a weight on their shoulders. And they were—the weight of guilt on their consciences. As for the point about rewarding our kids for telling the truth, I have a story that illustrates this. When my son Josh was six years old, he was playing in the backyard one day. Our backyard was mix of grass, a swimming pool, and a desertscape of decorative rocks. It was a warm Saturday afternoon, and I was watching a college football game in the house when there was a knock on our door. It was our next-door neighbor, and I could tell he wasn't happy. "Hey, uh, can you come over to my house? I need to show you something."

"Okay" I replied, wondering what he wanted to show me. He led me into his backyard, where he also had a pool. The difference between his pool and my pool was that the bottom of his pool was covered with desertscape decorative rocks. I mean, the whole bottom of his pool. There were hundreds of rocks. Amazingly, they looked just like the rocks in my yard. How cool. What a coincidence—wait a minute! My neighbor then proceeded to tell me when he came home from running errands he saw handfuls of rocks flying from my yard into his pool. Yep, my six-year-old son was throwing rocks from my yard, over the fence, into his pool. Josh! I apologized and immediately went to my house to have a talk with the boy. I took Josh out into our backyard to a place where there seemed to be a few rocks missing. "Josh, did you throw rocks over the fence into the neighbor's pool?" I thought it was important for him to confess and tell the truth, since I hadn't actually seen him do it. I'll never forget his response.

He twisted his face up a little bit and said, "If I tell the truth, will I get in trouble?"

He had me there. I had to respond, "Well, Josh, if you tell Dad the truth, you won't get into trouble, because telling the truth is important. But we will go over and help clean up the mess you made."

"Okay," he said sheepishly. "I did it."

I responded as any loving, gentle father would: "HOW COULD YOU DO SOMETHING LIKE THIS, YOU LITTLE HEATHEN CHILD, AND WHO IS YOUR MOTHER

ANYWAY!" No, that's not how I responded. I thanked him for telling me the truth. I told him I loved him, was proud of him for being honest, and asked him to never do it again. A bond of trust was being built that has lasted to this day. Josh and our daughters have all come to us to confess things in honesty, because they know we value honesty and will reward them for it. As a side note, I was later sharing the funny story of Josh throwing rocks into my neighbor's pool with the neighbor who lived on the other side of me. He started laughing and told me that on the same day he heard, "what I thought were cats fighting on my roof. I came outside and saw your son Josh throwing rocks onto my roof." I looked down where I was standing and noticed a few rocks were missing from this side of the yard too. Later I asked Josh why he'd thrown the rocks in the first place. He said it was because he liked the sound they made when they landed in the water and on the tile roof. If you've ever had a six-year-old son, you'll know this makes perfect sense!

Honor

I touched on the principle of honor in regards to the way we connect with our spouse in the area of conversation in chapter 5. I want to now apply the honor principle to raising children. The Bible teaches children to honor their parents in Ephesians 6:2-3 (NIV) "Honor your father and mother"—which is the first commandment with a promise—so that it may go well with you and that you may enjoy a long life on earth." The key here is that the *value* a person places on another is the choice of the person doing the valuing. It's subjective, because it's according to the person's character or station in life. Would we place as much honor on a known criminal as on a police officer? No. Would we place as much honor on a lazy person who can't keep a job as on a diligent entrepreneur who owns a successful business? No. Would we place as much honor on a person who is a proven liar as on someone who we know is honest and tells the truth? No. But what if the criminal, the lazy person, or the liar was our parent, sibling, or child? We certainly wouldn't honor their actions, but we would honor them at some level for the fact that they are family members. The point is that honor is subjective to the person it is being placed on. Pastor Larry Stockstill defines honor as looking past the person to the office or position that they hold.

So, in light of what we know about honor, who do we train our children to honor? The first and most important person children need to honor is God. Children learn to honor God by the way we, as their parents, speak about him and how we live our lives for him. By seeing their parents reading the Bible, praying together as a family, and worshipping in church on a regular basis, our children learn how important God is. When children observe that God is first in our lives, it's easy for them to make him first in their lives. Honoring God creates a culture in our homes that penetrates the hearts of children, especially when they are young. By watching their parents honor God in their lives, they will learn to honor God with theirs.

Now, I have a special note regarding older children and honoring God. As children grow older, they will go through the inevitable and important process of making their faith their own. This involves questioning their faith, the Bible, and spiritual authority. Parents need to recognize this and let it happen. Children mature spiritually at different ages and stages of life. Sometimes they go sideways and involve themselves in destructive behaviors that sadden God and make us angry or afraid. We've had seasons like this with our own children. What to do? Pray for them like crazy. Love them unconditionally. Don't push them away because of the choices they are making. They need you on their team more than ever. What we have discovered time and time again is that if you maintain your relationship with them during these hard times, they will come back to you and to God. God never left them or turned his back on them. And parents shouldn't either. Grace and unconditional love is what God is all about. Parents should do their best to model this to their wayward kids. Just know that love and acceptance is what brings kids back to you and to God. Romans 2:4 in the New Living Translation describes this perfectly, "Don't you see how wonderfully kind, tolerant and patient God is with you? Does this mean nothing to you? Can't you see that his kindness is intended to turn you from your sin?" The NIV translation says, "Or do you show contempt for the riches of his kindness, forbearance, and patience, not realizing that God's kindness is intended to lead you to repentance?" Does this mean parents should turn a blind eye and allow sinful behavior in the home? No, but in dealing with children and teens who are not honoring God, it's always most effective when these issues are cloaked in love and kindness.

The second group of people children need to honor is their family. It's important that children and teens show respect for Mom and Dad and their siblings, as well as extended family. Honor is shown by the way family members speak to and interact with one another. Parents should allow some playful teasing but not hurtful words that can wound hearts. Siblings can devastate each other with their words. Teasing, ridicule, and put-downs can cause great damage to a brother or sister's emotional state, which can affect their view of themselves and their future. Many times, things siblings have said to them stay with a person until adulthood. Honor is shown by siblings building each other up and protecting each other from hurtful words.

As well, parents should not tolerate rebellious, angry words spoken to them from their children. Kids need to learn how to communicate respectfully, showing honor to their parents. Yelling, screaming, and outright disobedience/defiance fall under the category of not showing honor and shouldn't be tolerated. I cringe every time I hear a child speaking disrespectfully to parents and the parents simply taking it, as if they have no control over the situation. The child is learning that it's okay to speak this way to Mom and Dad, and the path is cleared for a life of disrespect. I've heard parents say out of frustration, "I love my child, but I don't like him" because of this issue. Well, whose fault is that? Parents, be strong, and teach your children how to show respect to their family. Remember that you are modeling this for your children. If you put your spouse down, yell, make fun of each other, or call names, then chances are that your children will become just like you. But if they live in a home where tempers are under control, loving and encouraging words are spoken between Mom and Dad, and respect for others is part of the culture in the family, then the chances are greater that your children will grow up to be close friends to each other and to you. Trust me, that is what you want. It warms my heart when I see our adult children still being the best of friends.

The third group of people children need to honor are those in civil authority. Honoring authority is becoming a lost concept in current culture. All levels of authority are attacked through social media channels like Twitter, Facebook, Snapchat, and blogs. Anybody can write something disrespectful and dishonoring of someone in authority at any time and send it out to the social media sphere to be read by countless people. Cable television political-opinion shows are full of dishonorable statements, discussions, and name-calling of our nation's leaders. Students are now used to calling teachers and bosses by their first names instead of

Mr., Ms., Miss, or Mrs. Culture changes, and I get that. I'm not suggesting we go back to the days of "Yes, sir," and "Yes, ma'am." But there are people of authority that children need to honor. Civil authority would include law enforcement officers, holders of political office, and our military. Schoolteachers, employers, and coaches are all authorities whom children should learn to honor.

What if these people are bad people? Should our kids still honor them? Yes. Remember that honor is a subjective value placed on another. Let's say an employer doesn't treat your son very well at the ice cream store where he works. He's critical, a bit mean, and angry. Your son doesn't have to honor him as a good man, but he should honor him for the position of authority he has as his boss. See how that works? You don't have to like the president of the United States, but you should still honor the office he or she holds as the leader of our country. As we honor those in authority, we honor God. Paul writes in Romans 13:1–5, "Let everyone be subject to the governing authorities, for there is no authority except that which God has established. The authorities that exist have been established by God. Consequently, whoever rebels against the authority is rebelling against what God has instituted, and those who do so will bring judgment on themselves. For rulers hold no terror for those who do right, but for those who do wrong. Do you want to be free from fear of the one in authority? Then do what is right and you will be commended. For the one in authority is God's servant for your good. But if you do wrong, be afraid, for rulers do not bear the sword for no reason. They are God's servants, agents of wrath to bring punishment on the wrongdoer. Therefore, it is necessary to submit to the authorities, not only because of possible punishment but also as a matter of conscience." The principle here is that we need to honor what God has established. This is a valuable lesson for kids.

Lastly, there is spiritual authority. Pastors, youth leaders, kid ministry leaders, and Bible teachers all fall under this category. God has placed people in positions of spiritual authority in local churches in order to help people grow and mature in spiritual, as well as practical, matters of life. Parents must model this for their children, to show the importance of having spiritual authority in our lives. Are you submitted to spiritual authority? Do you honor the leaders of your local church? How do you talk about the pastor of your church in front of the kids? What you say will go a long way in determining how your children view spiritual authority. Are you critical of decisions you disagree with? Do you ridicule your spiritual leaders and disrespect them with your humor? Or do you speak highly of them and honor them in front of your children?

As a pastor, I can speak for all of us when I say that we don't do everything right. We make bad decisions at times and say foolish and inappropriate things from the pulpit once in a while. We offend and hurt people. We are human. And it's okay to come to us and let us know if we've offended you or if you disagree with a decision and want to discuss it. I'm not saying spiritual authority is perfect and shouldn't be questioned, challenged, or even corrected at times. But how you do it and how you present issues like this in front of your children makes a big difference in how they will grow up viewing spiritual authority. Trust me, you want your children to honor spiritual authority, because that very authority will help them have fruitful, productive lives, solid relationships, and emotional and spiritual health. But this will happen only if spiritual authority is honored and received with respect. The person who wrote the letter to the Hebrews in the New Testament wrote the following statement: "Obey your spiritual leaders, and do what they say. Their work is to watch over your souls, and they are accountable to God. Give them reason to do this with joy and not with sorrow. That would certainly not be for your benefit" (Hebrews 13:17, NLT).

Children who give honor will become people of honor.

Humility

Humility lives in a place between pride and low self-esteem. It means being confident without being cocky. It's not thinking more highly of ourselves than we should, while at the same time not thinking lower of ourselves than we should. Humility is having an accurate perspective of our strengths and abilities as well as self-awareness and acceptance of our natural weaknesses and limitations. Nobody is perfect, and our kids need to know that is okay.

To instill humility in our children is to teach them to love people. Loving people is simply accepting people from all walks of life and seeing people as God's creation, having value and adding to the beauty and fabric of the world. Loving people means looking for the good and hoping for the best in others. (Now, it is very important that you also teach your children to have wisdom and discernment in regards to recognizing those who would try to hurt them or others, or who are dishonest, lack integrity, or engage in destructive behaviors. So, yes, there is a balance.)

To instill humility in our children is to teach them to serve people. Nothing is more humbling than serving others less fortunate. Sacrificing time, energy, and resources to lift others up and meet a need is an incredible show of humility. Serving helps children remain grateful for what they have instead of unhappy about what they don't have. Serving lets our children know that life is more about others than themselves. Jesus was a great example in serving others. He humbly met people's physical needs, mixed socially with the under-resourced, fed the hungry, comforted those hurting, and prayed for others. He meant what he said when he described himself as a man who "did not come be served, but to serve" (Matthew 20:28). I encourage you to find ways to get your children involved in age-appropriate opportunities to serve others. Whether it's handing out food at an outreach, visiting sick kids in the hospital, or helping fellow students with homework, serving others will keep them humble.

One last point on humility. One of the humblest things a person can do is encourage people. When self-centeredness takes over, children focus their thoughts and conversation around themselves. When they take the focus off their own lives, wants, and desires and place their focus onto lifting up someone else's life, this is an act of humility. Teach your children to encourage others by using kind words. Kindness lifts people's spirits. Kindness warms people's hearts. Kindness melts away negative feelings other kids have about themselves.

As I mentioned earlier in this chapter, God's kindness toward us is what drew us to him and caused us to respond to his grace and see our lives changed (Romans 2:4). Your child's kindness can change a life too!

Honesty, honor, and humility will take your children far in life. They will gain respect from others, they will receive honor because they are giving honor, and they will have many life-giving relationships because humility is irresistible and many people will want to be their friends.

Chapter 18

The Wins

When playing the game of life (real life, not Life the board game), it's important to know what you are playing for. The motivation to keep playing is known as *the win*. The win is the big payoff. The win is the "what's in it for you." The win is the *why* of "Why did you go through child-raising?" In other words, what do you want the end result to be when your children launch and leave home as adults? Here are *the wins*.

Win #1: Their will is submitted to God's will.

A child's will is the land of free choice. It is of utmost importance that we as parents train our children to obey God's Word and God's voice. Psalm 119:9 answers a question all parents have: "How can a young person stay on the path of purity? By living according to your word." Training our kids to align their practical everyday lives to the Bible's instruction is key to their success in life. Obedience to God's Word is the world's most secure safety net. It's the manual, the blueprint, the prescription for a healthy life. Living life aligned to God's Word brings blessing beyond measure. We must teach this to our kids.

Obeying God's voice is a little trickier but super powerful. The voice of God is the still, small voice in our hearts that leads and guides us in life through the Holy Spirit. The Holy Spirit lives in us (Romans 8:9; 1 Corinthians 3:16; 1 John 2:27). One of his main roles is to speak to us and lead us into truth (John 16:13). The Holy Spirit also gives us practical direction for our lives (Romans 8:29). Just as the voice of your GPS app speaks to you while you are driving, giving you directions to your desired destination, so does the Holy Spirit. Teaching your children that the Holy Spirit lives in them and speaks to them helps them obey the "feeling" or the "leading" they feel in their hearts. The voice speaking to them about what to do and what not to do is the Holy Spirit helping them make a right choice or a proper response in a given situation. It is subjective, but as they learn to listen to the voice of God through the Holy Spirit, they will be able to avoid many pitfalls.

How do children learn to submit to God's Word and God's voice? By watching their parents submit to God's Word and God's voice. When they see you making decisions according to what the Bible says, or praying first before taking action, they see in real time how to submit a will to God's will.

Children also learn this by experiencing and responding to parental discipline. As children learn to obey their parents, they learn to obey God.[1] Unfortunately for the kids, they were born with a sinful nature, and discipline is unavoidable. Parental discipline is an earthly example of God's spiritual discipline. And the way children respond to their parent's discipline will determine how they respond to God's discipline as they mature. Hebrews 12:5–10 (NIV) says, "And have you completely forgotten this word of encouragement that addresses you as a father addresses his son? It says, 'My son, do not make light of the Lord's discipline, and do not lose heart when he rebukes you, because the Lord disciplines the one he loves, and he hastens everyone he accepts as his son.' Endure hardship as discipline; God is treating you as his children. For what children are not disciplined by their father? If you are not disciplined—and everyone undergoes discipline—then you are not legitimate, not true sons and daughters at all. Moreover, we have all had human fathers who disciplined us and we respected them for it. How much more should we submit to the Father of spirits and live! They disciplined us for a little while as they thought best; but God disciplines us for our good, in order that we may share in his holiness."

Parental and Godly discipline is good for us. That's right. Just like spinach. I hate spinach. I hate discipline. But I like the results of both. The result of discipline is that rebellion is removed from our hearts, and that becomes *the* key is submitting our will to God's will. Rebellion is the worship of our own opinion in place of worshipping God and his opinion. It's *me-first* living, and it drives us to destructive behaviors that ruin our lives. Rebellion is submitting to our own wills instead of God's will. What saves us and reverses this course? Discipline. Rebellion in the heart of a child diminishes when through a parent's discipline they learn to submit to God, obeying his Word and following the voice of the Holy Spirit.

I will cover child discipline in more detail in chapter 19. But for now, just know that as a parent you would be wise to discipline your children; it will help them get their will submitted to God's will.

When I now see my adult kids living out their relationships and shaping their financial strategies according to how the Bible instructs them to, I feel a sense of relief. They will be okay, because they are doing things God's way. When I hear how they pray about decisions they are making and are listening for God's leading, I know that they will come out on top. That is a wonderful *win*.

Win #2: We become friends when they reach adulthood.

I love being friends with my adult children. We share common interests. We enjoy being together. We go to concerts, watch movies together, and play games together as friends. This dynamic relationship shift comes into play as children graduate high school and become adults. You will parent less and become more of a friend. A friend supports, encourages, and is available when challenges hit. This is not at all an attempt to water down your role as parent. That will always exist. The change comes in how it exists. You begin the process when your children enter their late teens. The friendship process begins by allowing them more freedom to make decisions for themselves. The friendship continues by you allowing them to suffer the consequences for any bad choices they make, while at the same time letting them know you love them unconditionally. The friendship process comes full circle with you providing solid counsel, yet letting them make decisions that affect their lives and future, such as higher education, career, and relationship choices.

One of the huge challenges that comes during this transition from parent to friend is in maintaining relationships during challenging times due to unwise choices. When our kids are making unwise life choices and participating in behaviors contrary to God's word, we have to ask ourselves the question, "Is our response to their behavior worth breaking off our relationship with our child?" In other words, are your strong feelings about their choices more important than your relationship with them? Is it worth being "right" and risking breaking your friendship by pushing them away? Or is it better to allow them to make adult decisions, even though they are wrong and harmful, cover them with grace and unconditional love, and maintain a loving relationship? Over the years we've learned that maintaining the relationship is key to them eventually coming to their senses and making positive changes.

When children know they are accepted and are able to come back home and seek support from Dad and Mom, the healing and restoration process begins sooner and takes a shorter amount of time to achieve. If the relationship is broken and can't be repaired because of anger or rejection, they will look to other people for support and help, leaving their parents outside their circle. You are then left out of the loop and will have the difficult task of attempting to reconcile your relationship. That is not easy. Watching children grow up and abuse alcohol or drugs, participate in sexual activity outside of marriage with the opposite gender or the same gender, marry the wrong person, make bad financial decisions, or walk away from their faith in God can cause feelings of anger, disappointment, and bitterness in our hearts. This results in separation. We have to "guard our heart" (Proverbs 4:23) against these. We must cover them in unconditional love because "love covers over a multitude of sin" (1 Peter 4:8), and we must receive them with open arms when they come back and ask for help.

Jesus tells the fictional story about the lost son. Even though the story isn't a *true* story, it is a *truth* story. And it's powerful.

> Jesus continued: "There was a man who had two sons. The younger one said to his father, 'Father, give me my share of the estate.' So he divided his property between them.
> "Not long after that, the younger son got together all he had, set off for a distant country and there squandered his wealth in wild living. After he had spent everything, there was a severe famine in that whole country, and he began to be in need. So he went

and hired himself out to a citizen of that country, who sent him to his fields to feed pigs. He longed to fill his stomach with the pods that the pigs were eating, but no one gave him anything.

"When he came to his senses, he said, 'How many of my father's hired servants have food to spare, and here I am starving to death! I will set out and go back to my father and say to him: Father, I have sinned against heaven and against you. I am no longer worthy to be called your son; make me like one of your hired servants.' So he got up and went to his father.

"But while he was still a long way off, his father saw him and was filled with compassion for him; he ran to his son, threw his arms around him and kissed him.

"The son said to him, 'Father, I have sinned against heaven and against you. I am no longer worthy to be called your son.'

"But the father said to his servants, 'Quick! Bring the best robe and put it on him. Put a ring on his finger and sandals on his feet. Bring the fattened calf and kill it. Let's have a feast and celebrate. For this son of mine was dead and is alive again; he was lost and is found.' So they began to celebrate.

"Meanwhile, the older son was in the field. When he came near the house, he heard music and dancing. So he called one of the servants and asked him what was going on. 'Your brother has come,' he replied, 'and your father has killed the fattened calf because he has him back safe and sound.'

"The older brother became angry and refused to go in. So his father went out and pleaded with him. But he answered his father, 'Look! All these years I've been slaving for you and never disobeyed your orders. Yet you never gave me even a young goat so I could celebrate with my friends. But when this son of yours who has squandered your property with prostitutes comes home, you kill the fattened calf for him!'

"'My son,' the father said, 'you are always with me, and everything I have is yours'" (Luke 15:11—31 NIV).

This story is not just about a son who disrespected his father, took an early inheritance, wasted it on the party life, and then returned home broken and bruised. This story is also about a loving father who accepted his son's bad decisions, welcomed him home with open arms, and reconciled their relationship. In verse 17, the son "came to his senses." That is the key phrase in this story. There was a time in our own lives when we came to our senses and made life-altering decisions. You remember that, right? It was when we gave our lives to Christ, stopped partying, broke up bad relationships, joined a church, ate better and improved our health, got our finances in order, or whatever the circumstances were—we changed. Just so the son came to his senses and realized that the life he was leading had ended up being worse than living at home. He knew that the servants working in his father's house were better off than he was. So he decided to come home. The father, in verse 20, was looking for his return: "But while he was still a long way off, his father saw him and was filled with compassion for him; he ran to his son, threw his arms around him and kissed him." This verse is challenging for many of us. I know what it is to be up at night as a concerned parent praying for our children. I know how it feels when you catch them participating in destructive behavior, and the anger, the disappointment and the fear that grips your emotions. And yet, I see from this story that the proper response for me as a father is to look for them when they are far off, to run to them when they turn toward home, and to love them and to show compassion as their hearts return home. It's difficult sometimes. If this story was written about me as the father, verse 20 would say, "He ran to his son, put his hands around his neck, and strangled him"—not really. But as parents we want to judge them, berate them, and make them feel guilty for what they put us through and for making such stupid choices. What Jesus is describing in this story is how my heavenly Father receives me when I make wrong choices. When I fall short and deserve his wrath, he gives me love and compassion. When I disappoint, his grace and mercy are extended to me. When I, like the lost son, say to God that I'm not worthy to be called his son and not worthy to be used by him, he cuts me off and throws a party in my honor (verses 22, 23). It's a story of grace, forgiveness, and redemption.

This is when our true love is shown, when we love our children during both the good and the bad times. It's when we stick with them even when it's hard and they pull away. Proverbs 17:17 says, "A friend loves at all times, and a brother is born for a time of adversity." As parents, we need to love our children at all times and be there for them in times of adversity.

Win #3: They know how to make wise decisions.

All parents have a common dream for their children. The dream is that they will be successful in every area of life. We want them to be happy. We want them to be healthy. We want them to prosper financially. We want them to be fulfilled in their endeavors. We want them to have a higher quality of life than we have. We want them to avoid the mistakes that we made. And we want them to avoid the painful lessons of failure that we experienced. This is a great dream, a high goal to achieve, but most likely pretty unrealistic in all of these areas. Our children will leave our homes and wrestle with life as it comes. They will win some battles and lose some battles. As parents we can help to set them up for the greatest probability for success by teaching them the value of *wisdom*. Wisdom is key for winning in every area of life. Wisdom comes in three packages.

First, wisdom comes from God, through prayer and his Word, the Bible. Second, wisdom comes through learning from others. Learning from others comes through reading; attending classes, seminars, workshops, or church services; mentoring relationships; and listening to experts and preachers on podcasts. Third, wisdom is attained through making mistakes. I personally prefer the first two. I'd rather glean wisdom from God himself and from others who have gone before me and know more than I do. I like learning from others' mistakes instead of my own. Unfortunately for me, the third option has been a common teacher in the area of wisdom. So, as a parent, I want to teach my children to value wisdom, to learn how to attain it and then implement it in their lives.

The word *wisdom* is found in the Bible over 220 times. It is a major theme and is always connected to making right choices and succeeding in life.

There was a man mentioned briefly in the Bible in Exodus 31, named Bezalel. He possessed what I strive for and what I want instilled in my children. "I have chosen Bezalel … and I have filled him with the Spirit of God, with wisdom, and understanding, and knowledge and with all kinds of skills" (Exodus 31:1–3 NIV). In this verse, the Hebrew word for *wisdom* means to "have good sense." We all want our children to grow up having good sense when it comes to choices, relationships, finances, and attitudes. The word *understanding* means to have a "God-given perception of the nature and meaning of things, resulting in sound judgment and decision-making; in particular, the ability to discern spiritual truth and to apply it to human disposition and conduct."[2] Wisdom is more a head condition. It's the ability to make a good decision based on the facts presented. Understanding is more a condition of the heart. Its descriptors are "perception," "discern," "spiritual in nature." God grants us understanding, which would be his point of view on the subject. I want my kids to know how God feels about things they are considering. *Knowledge* is from the Hebrew root word *yada*, which indicates a "knowing by seeing." Knowledge is more visual. Knowledge comes by looking at something, reading something, or seeing an illustration or demonstration. So if we combine all of these together, we see that Godly wisdom is a combination of having common sense, spiritual discernment, and the ability to visually see things as they should be. If a person possesses all three of these, then like Bezalel, they will have many *skills.* And having many skills leads a person to success. In which areas of life should parents impart wisdom to their children?

Spiritual Decisions

Leading our children to a place where they develop a personal relationship with God, by asking Jesus into their lives to become their Lord and Savior, is the most significant thing we can do for our kids, no matter what their ages. By accepting Jesus and becoming Christ-followers, they will not only secure places in eternity with God when it's their time to meet him face to face but they will also benefit from the "abundant life" that God has for them here on earth, as Jesus describes.[3] This is what all of us want for our precious children. Now, it's important to remember that we can't make their decisions for them. We can't force them to come to faith in Christ. But we can lead them to the place of decision by attending a strong local church that has the resources and skilled leadership to provide our children an incredible kids' ministry experience as well as student ministry for junior and senior high school kids. If your current church doesn't have a strong option for you and your family, then you need to find a church that does. This is critical to your child's spiritual development.

You should also model for your children what it means to have a personal relationship with Jesus. Let your kids see you pray, read the Bible, attend a small group, and go to church on a consistent basis. Let them hear you talk about what God has done for your family and how much you love him and are grateful for his saving you and healing your life. Proverbs 111:10 says, "The fear of the Lord is the foundation of true wisdom, all who obey his commands will grow in wisdom" (NLT). The word *fear* means to have awe and respect for God, not to actually be afraid or fearful of him in the sense of how you are afraid at horror movies. So you can see clearly that having a relationship with God is where wisdom starts. It's the foundation or building block for success in life.

Relational Decisions

When our kids were little, I would tell them (with a smile and a wink) that their mother and I were the "bosses of their lives" and that we would determine who their friends would be. We were very involved in who they made friends with. There were times when we had to put the kibosh on a friend or two. When we noticed that a friend's influence wasn't pulling our kid in the right direction, we would step in and end the friendship. If we saw that after spending time with a certain child our kid had a bad attitude toward us or a bit of rebellion toward authority, we would step in and begin to sever that friendship. We would first sit our kid down and let him or her know what negative traits we saw as a result of the friendship with that person, and we would explain why we were making this decision to not let them continue the relationship on a close-friend level. We then never allowed them to hang out with that friend for long periods of time (or at all, in extreme cases). Were some of their parents upset or offended? Yes. But our kids' attitude, emotional, and behavioral condition, as well as their future, was at stake. So it was worth it.

Helping your children pick the right friends is so very important. When your children are under the age of ten, it's important to pick children to become their close friends who respect authority, obey their parents, get along with others, have a positive attitude, and share many of the important values you have as a family.

Between the ages of ten and thirteen was when it got a bit dicey for us. This is the age when friends who don't share your child's faith can shipwreck it. This is the age when exposure to pornography on a friend's phone or computer can happen. This is the age when inappropriate movies can be watched in the home of a friend who doesn't share your values. One of our family standards was that whenever a movie was going to be shown at a friend's house, our kids would call or text us first and tell us which movie was going to be shown. I would look at a Christian values-based website that gives detailed movie reviews, including all detailed sexual scenes and profanity counts. I'd then make a judgment call. Yes, sometimes I did have to drive over and pick up our son or daughters because I didn't want them exposed to what was going to be shown. Was it challenging for us to do that? You bet. It wasn't fun for our kids either. But doing this saved them from seeing something they shouldn't see, and it helped them to see what wisdom looks like when it comes to what we allow ourselves to view and how to make wise entertainment choices. And looking into the future, when they have their own children in similar circumstances, they will at least know a good option as it was modeled by us.

The ages of fourteen to eighteen present a whole new world. I remember turning the corner onto the cul-de-sac we lived on and seeing a young girl in a barely-there bikini riding her bike in circles in front of my house. She was a "friend" of my son's and wanted him to come over to hang out. Move along, little missy. Helping your teenagers make wise relational decisions is a huge challenge and not for the faint of heart. But be strong you must! The same principles applied to our kids when they were teenagers as when they were six years old. But the consequences for a bad relational decision were much costlier. Every family is different, and our standards might not be what you think would be best for your family. But here are some relationship principles we lived by when our kids became teenagers.

- Before you can go to the house of someone we don't know, we need to meet them first.
- You can't spend the night at anyone's house that we don't approve.
- Mom and Dad have all access to your phone/mobile devices at any time.
- You will turn in your phone to us at bedtime. You'll get it back in the morning.
- No computers or TVs in the bedroom. Ever.
- No dating relationships allowed while you're in high school.

Sound strict? Parenting together takes strong parents willing to lay the law down to keep their teens out of trouble and to teach them wisdom. Bad relationships destroy lives. The cost is too much for a huge mistake. Our biggest regret in raising our teenagers was the times we gave in to our kids' pressure and violated our own parenting standards. I remember with one of our kids, I gave in and let them spend the night with a group of friends that we didn't know. "They are all good kids, Dad."

"Okay. I trust you." Big mistake. Later, when my teenager confessed what had really gone on that night, I felt sick to my stomach. I had let my guard down. I paid for it and my teenage child paid for it when I allowed them to go somewhere I knew in my heart I shouldn't have. It was a lesson learned the hard way. Teach your children the value of wisdom in relationships.

Financial Decisions

When money gets tight—or worse, goes away—then life gets hard. Money problems are a huge issue and are a major reason that couples get divorced. Debt can cause deep discouragement leading to depression. Unpaid bills can cause health issues, as our bodies react chemically to the stress of worrying about them.

Parenting together should include both Dad and Mom talking to their children about money. Here are some principles we've taught our kids.

- The first 10 percent belongs to God. We believe the Bible teaches tithing (*tithe* means "tenth") as a principle to live by. We taught our kids to give a dime for every dollar they earned to our local church. Scripture is clear that this pleases God and brings with it his blessing. Even during a personal financial crisis, we brought to God a tithe. He turned things around for us, and we are back in the land of blessings.

- The next 10 percent belongs to your savings account. The next dime of every dollar went into savings accounts we opened for our kids when they started earning money consistently.

- Stay out of debt. There are different opinions about the topic of debt and its proper use. We taught our kids to pay cash for everything. The one exception is that we encouraged our kids to go to college and gave our blessings to accumulate *reasonable* amounts of college debt in order to prepare for solid careers.

- Invest for your retirement. Once their careers began, we taught them to enroll in their company retirement plans and auto-deduct a percentage of their salary into the plan. If young adults in their twenties will invest two hundred dollars a month into a 401(k) or similar plan and do that for their whole careers, they will be millionaires by the time they reach retirement age.

- Give generously to others. We live our financial lives with an open hand. We tithe, but we also give above and beyond the tithe. The Bible gives numerous promises to those who live a life of generosity, and so we support missions, church building projects, individuals in need, and community service projects that help people who are under-resourced. Look at these promises to the generous: "Give freely and become more wealthy; be stingy and lose everything" (Proverbs 11:24 NLT). "The generous will prosper; those who refresh others will themselves be refreshed" (Proverbs 11:25 NLT). "If you help the poor, you are lending to the Lord and he will repay you!" (Proverbs 19:17 NLT).

- It's all about the percentages. Lifestyle is limited by the boundaries of income. So instead of thinking in terms of dollars, we taught our kids to think in terms of percentages. You start with 100 percent. You give God 10 percent. You give your savings account 10 percent. You give your retirement account 1 to 5 percent, and you keep breaking it down per item until you are at 0 percent. Help them set up a monthly budget based on the percentages, and each month should work for them financially. Play the percentages, and your kids should end up spending less than they bring home each month.

- Ask for financial advice. When deciding to make a large purchase, like a car or home, or when looking at an investment opportunity, it's always good to get another set of eyes looking at the financial aspect to make sure it's sound and solid. It is worth seeking wise counsel in order to avoid making big, costly mistakes. Seek out real estate professionals, automotive professionals, financial advisors, or businesspeople. Encourage your kids to develop relationships with people in the know so that when they are faced with a big decision they have the resources they need to collect pertinent data and look objectively at the financial opportunity.

I remember talking to a mature woman who had raised two children, both of whom were succeeding in their young adult lives. I asked her if she thought there was any area of parenting in which she and her husband had fallen short. (I'm not afraid to ask these kinds of questions, because I want to learn from others' mistakes as well as their victories.) She gave the following reply: "I wish we would have given our kids a greater perspective on the value of a dollar. We made life too easy for them when it came to material things, and now that they are adults, they are having to learn some difficult lessons in the area of spending."

If you, as the parents, struggle in the area of money management, then seek out help for yourselves, and bring your children into the conversation, so they can learn right beside you. As they see you getting advice and making adjustments, that will inspire them to do the same someday.

When finances are in order, then there is room for peace to reign supreme in the home. Parenting together is much easier when your finances are on solid ground. Teach your children how to build their finances on the same solid ground, and they'll experience the same peace in their own households someday. That is a great gift to give them as they move out of your home and into their own.

Win #4: They marry the right person.

Speaking of big decisions, this is the biggest of them all. Helping your adult children decide on whether the person they are considering for marriage is the right one is a great service that we as parents provide. When my oldest daughter was still too young to date, I convinced myself that I would rejoice when she finally met her guy. Not true. Didn't happen. After high school graduation, when young men started hanging around and pursuing her, I noticed that my natural response was the opposite of rejoicing. It was protecting her from the idiotic boys who actually thought they were good enough for her. Who did they think they were?

After a couple of false starts, she eventually did meet Mr. Right, and she and Tim were married. My natural defense mechanism was worn down by his charm, character, and love for

God. Tim is a great son-in-law, and I'm happy to include him in our family. He is a *win*.

How can parents help their children prepare to make the biggest decision of their lives?

First, as soon as you find out you are having a baby, begin to pray for his or her future spouse. Both Autumn and I have spent years praying for the future spouses of our children. As of this writing, one out of our four kids is married, but I can say that God answered our prayers, because our son-in-law, Tim, is a perfect fit for our daughter Rachel. We continue to pray that God will bring the right person into the lives of our remaining unmarried children.

Second, when our kids were in junior high we would reaffirm that there was to be no dating anyone seriously until they graduated from high school. We would teach them that dating was reserved for the age and time when they could actually get married if they did meet someone they liked. High school was a time for having lots of friends of both genders without the stress and pressure of premature romance—not to mention the temptation for sexual sin. One big mistake parents of teenagers make is allowing, promoting, and even instigating romantic relationships for their children while they are still in high school. Emotionally they just aren't ready; financially they aren't ready; and morally they aren't ready for serious romance. I was a youth pastor for many years, and I've seen many teenage lives messed up emotionally and morally because of romantic relationships that they weren't mature enough to navigate while in high school. The saddest part? The parents who thought it was "cute," "sweet," and "fun" were promoting something that their kids weren't equipped or mature enough to handle.

Third, begin coaching your children in what to look for in a future spouse at a young age. About twelve years of age is a good time to start "sowing seeds" of wisdom into your child regarding what to look for in a future spouse. We would talk openly about how important it is to marry a person with the right character, attitude, and habits. We would point out young couples in our church who had married rightly and would let our kids know what their relationship had looked like leading up to their marriage. Our kids would have questions, and we would honestly answer them to help them process and develop the right marriage mind-set, even at their young ages. The big idea here is that you want your children to have a mature perspective on marriage at a young age, so they can see through culture's lies about young love and sexual hookups before marriage.

Fourth, when they were in high school, we would get more specific about what to look for in a future spouse. Here is a short list of characteristics that apply to both men and women:

- They love Jesus passionately.
- They are committed and involved in a strong local church.
- They exhibit mature characteristics, like honesty, caring for others, and kindness to others. They are not given to bouts of anger or moodiness, nor are they clingy or possessive. They are fun, have a positive attitude, and are motivated to accomplish something in life.
- They share spiritual dreams, financial dreams, and dreams of future children. Being aligned in these three areas builds a strong foundation to a good marriage.
- We encouraged our daughters to look for men who proactively pursued them. The logic was that if a young man sees a girl that he wants and pursues her, then he'll also pursue a career that he wants, a ministry that he wants, the material things that he wants. Autumn and I see this as a positive quality in a husband for our

daughters. We discourage our daughters from pursuing young men and asking them out, as popular as that is in today's culture. We also encourage them to guard their hearts and not give them away too fast—make the boys work a little bit. See what they are made of. Play hard to get until you know they are someone you are interested in. Once that is settled then, and only then, begin the process of developing a deeper relationship, and see where it goes.

- We encourage our son, Joshua, to actively pursue a young woman he wants to start dating. There is something about a young man who "mans up" and goes after what he wants. This translates not just to his future spouse but to all aspects of his life. If the woman is playing hard to get, then get a plan in place to overcome and wear her defenses down. Fight for her. Don't give up until you know for sure she's not interested. I'm not talking about stalking and annoying her, just pursuing gently until it's clear. Be a gentleman, and if she doesn't respond, then move on. But you never know until you try, and sometimes you have to try more than once.

- Lastly, we let our kids know that it is totally natural to want to date someone who you are physically attracted to. Physical attraction adds an element of fun and excitement. The whole attraction thing is subjective, of course. Sometimes a relationship starts as a friendship with no physical attraction but as a couple gets to know one another their friendship connection grows into a physical attraction, as they begin to notice little things about each other that they didn't notice before. I've had more than one conversation that went like this: "When I first met him, I wasn't attracted to him at all. But after I got to know him and how great of a guy he is, he became more attractive the longer we dated." I've had the opposite conversation as well. "She was so beautiful, but man, after I got to know her, I realized she wasn't the one for me." It's true that looks aren't everything, but they are something, and it's okay to date someone that you think is hot, a 10, or whatever term you want to use.

Helping your grown kids find their mates is a huge thing. Our job, really, is to train them how to pick a potential mate before they leave our homes and before they meet them. Once they are out of high school and of marrying age, then it's up to them. Hopefully they will filter all that they learned from you over the years and show enough wisdom and good judgment to actually date the right people.

Chapter 19

The Tools

As we come to the end of the parenting together section, I want to leave you with some tools that will help you in raising your children regardless of their age. It should be noted that there are various stages of child development that take different parenting approaches. I would recommend, if you are still a parent, that you purchase some resources that go more in depth than what I can do in this book on marriage.

But in general terms, here are five tools every parent can use in every stage of child raising.

Tool #1: Words You Speak Over Their Lives

In the chapter "Meaningful Conversation," I have written about the power of our words in the context of a married couple talking together. The same principal applies to parents and the way they speak to their children. Children, even more than adults, are sensitive to words spoken to them. God has created their young souls to be sensitive to his voice. In the same regard, they are sensitive to your voice. When you speak to them and let them know how much you love them, how proud you are of them, and what a bright future full of success and prosperity they have, they start to believe it. Your words can shape the trajectory of their lives and the direction of their destinies. Much of your children's self-esteem and confidence will come from your words. Their ability to overcome big challenges will be the result of your words of encouragement, wisdom, and motivation.

On the opposite end of the spectrum, when you use harsh language or speak angry words to your children, they feel it deeply, and their lives become much more difficult. Hurtful words can scar a child for life. Words that hurt are remembered far longer than words that encourage. As a pastor, I see this when I speak to people about God being a perfect father who is not angry at them but loves them unconditionally and forgives them totally. I see tears when I describe God as a heavenly Father who believes in them and wants to bless them in every area of life. They have never heard of a parent like that and find it almost too good to be true. I also see hesitation and skepticism in the faces of some, as they can't comprehend what a good parent is like, and they can't believe God really feels that way toward them. They can hardly believe that God is truly kind, loving, and not angry at them for their mistakes. They see God through the filter of their earthly parents who were mean, hurtful, and angry. I implore you not to be that way with your kids. Use kind words of encouragement and love. Lift them up and let them know you believe in them, just as God does.

This raises the question, is there ever a time when it is okay to be mad at your kids and to express that? Yes. There are times when corrective words need to be spoken to your kids. Absolutely. But there is a line that should never be crossed in those tense moments. And that line is the line of uncontrolled anger and hurtful correction that causes deep damage to their emotions. I've raised my voice numerous times to my children when they were doing something that could bring harm to themselves or others. I've been angry, frustrated, and tempted to say hurtful things to put them in their place or to make them feel stupid—as if that was going to help correct the behavior. Regretfully, sometimes I did give in to the urge. I want you to know I have failed miserably in this area with all of my children. I'm grateful that they've forgiven me and allowed me to apologize and reconcile with them. But even so, the scars and memories are still in there. As I matured as a parent (this is why I always tease our fourth child that she has it easy, compared to our first one), I learned to filter my words, and speak positive things over them even in corrective circumstances, and to always end the episode with words of love.

Tool #2: Time Spent Together

Time. Watching *The Sound of Music, Sense and Sensibility, Anne of Green Gables, Emma,* and the six-hour BBC version of *Pride and Prejudice* isn't exactly my definition of a good time. But it forced me to spend hours of couch time with my three daughters. They loved my inane questions and silly comments, especially about the men in those movies. I mean, really? C'mon. Man up. But I enjoyed the fact that they loved these movies so much that they quoted the lines, cried at the same place every time, and were so happy at the end when all worked out for everybody.

Time. My son, Joshua, played multiple sports from the time he was four years old through high school. I can't tell you how many hours I spent at practices, games, and backyard ball tosses. Literally hundreds. Maybe over a thousand. He was in football, baseball, and cross country—even wrestling, one year in high school. His first wrestling match was against a girl. How relieved I was when he pinned her and won. Whew!

Time. Hiking, biking, walking. Late night chats on the bed. Texts. Daddy/daughter dates. Daddy/son adventures.

Time. Vacations. Beach trips. Whale watching. Disneyland.

Time. Piano recitals. School choir concerts. Art class exhibits.

Time. Swimming. Skiing. Snowboarding. Boating.

Time. Bedtime stories. Dr. Seuss books. Tickle fights. Board games.

Time.

I'm actually tearing up a bit as I write these words because of all the memories I have of raising our kids. Spending time just being together is an investment in your kids that will pay great dividends. Time together increases conversation. Time together lowers defenses and facilitates relationship growth. Time together creates a bond of trust that reassures them that when things aren't going well, Mom and Dad will be there for them. Time together creates memories that last. Time together creates stories about the fun times and misadventures that you laugh about for years. Like the time when … oh, never mind. Time. Just being together. Time. It brings you close. And close is where you want to be.

Tool #3: Discipline

"Discipline your children while there is hope. Otherwise you will ruin their lives." Proverbs 19:18 (NLT)

"Direct your children onto the right path, and when they are older, they will not leave it." Proverbs 22:6 (NLT)

"A youngster's heart is filled with foolishness, but physical discipline will drive it far away." Proverbs 22:15 (NLT)

"Don't fail to discipline your children. They won't die if your spank them. Physical discipline may well save them from death." Proverbs 23:13–14 (NLT)

"Whoever spares the rod hates their children, but the one who loves their children is careful to discipline them." Proverbs 13:24 (NIV).

All children need discipline when their behavior warrants it. There are no exceptions to this rule (except for your children, I know. This section is for your neighbors). Discipline is the way to correct negative behaviors. Maturity and self-control will be gained in children who are properly disciplined by their parents. And let me insert this gentle reminder that God, our good, perfect, and loving heavenly Father, disciplines his adult children![1] That's you and me.

What are some behaviors that warrant discipline?

- Actions of defiance and disobedience toward authority
- Rebellious attitudes that poison the atmosphere of your home
- Hurtful words spoken with the motivation being to bring emotional pain to someone
- Purposeful physical harm afflicted on another person
- Lying

What are some effective methods of discipline? This is where it gets very subjective, because every child has a different emotional makeup. Some discipline methods work better than others on certain types of children. In our family, we used them all. We used time-outs, grounding, taking away favorite toys or electronics, and stern lectures. But the one method of discipline we used that was the most effective with all four of our children was spanking them. I still believe, especially with younger children aged two to eight, that controlled, nonabusive spanking is the most effective form of discipline. Let me give a brief defense for corporal punishment. No doubt, in recent years spanking has become controversial due to known extreme cases of very real physical abuse with angry, out-of-control parents hurting children unnecessarily. Of course, these are sad cases. Protection for the children should be the number-one priority, and proper authorities need to step in on those extreme cases. Spanking has also become controversial due to "research" papers that conclude that all spanking of children is "physiologically abusive" and "emotionally damaging" to children. There are forty-two world countries that have outlawed spanking altogether.[2] Should it be banned as a viable form of punishment for children? I think not. These extreme measures are overreactions to extreme cases. We found spanking is an effective way of dealing with behavior issues if administered correctly.

Why is spanking so effective? It's the Biblical method. "Don't fail to discipline your children. They won't die if your spank them. Physical discipline may well save them from death" (Proverbs 23:13–14 NLT). "Those who spare the rod of discipline hate their children. Those who love their children are careful to discipline them" (Proverbs 13:24 NLT).

Spanking also *immediately* addresses the situation. We found that time-outs didn't address the issue at hand when our kids were younger, because during time-outs kids just sat in a corner and thought about everything except what they'd done wrong. They looked at toys across the room; they thought about what they were going to do next or how badly they had to pee. Spanking causes children, under the guidance of loving parents, to think about what they did wrong and address it right that minute. They will then go through the healthy process of crying a few tears of repentance, which softens their hearts to their parents and to Jesus. Then they are open to receive a big hug and words of affirmation of love from Mom or Dad.

Most importantly, spanking opens their hearts to receive instruction, as well as closing them to the wrong that they committed. After the spanking, a lesson is taught, a prayer prayed, an apology offered, and forgiveness bestowed. And the best part is that once the episode is over, it's over. With a clear conscience, children feel better. The result? They can go play and be happy. Parents feel better because they were able to deal immediately with the issue and lead their child quickly through the discipline process instead of dragging it out for a long time.

Again, you know your child best. The reason I even bring up spanking is that in this generation of young parents I've noticed that fewer and fewer spank their kids, and they also wonder why their children are out of control. I can only speak from experience. We spanked all four of our children when they were little. Today they are emotionally healthy adults who don't harbor bitterness toward us or have any emotional scars because we spanked them. One thing I've learned over the years is that God knows what he's doing, and he gave us this instruction in the Bible. It works when done right, in love and not angrily or abusively.

Once kids get older, then other methods of discipline can be utilized to great effect. This is where you as the parent need to pray, discuss together, and get in agreement on what punishments will be used. We found our oldest daughter, Rachel, was strong willed, and we needed a stronger confrontation if we were to be effective. Our second daughter, Christina was tenderhearted and responsive, so a look and a strong conversation could do the trick. Our third child is our son, Josh, and he took our creative punishment development to whole new levels! Our last child, our baby, is Alyssa. And she is a unique balance of being strong willed yet very responsive to authority. Discipline was easily administered and readily accepted by her. Each of our kids was unique, and so we punished them uniquely. We prayed a lot and asked God for his wisdom and help. We sought the counsel of other parents, learned the ideas and methods that worked for them, and adopted some of them. You have to make it work for your own individual family members. I wish there were a one-size-fits-all method for discipline that would work for all kids everywhere. There's not. But there is a Holy Spirit, who will help you know what to do.

Tool #4: Failure and Mistakes

Life is hard, and we have to teach this truth to our kids. When they are young, we try to shelter them from pain and disappointment that life brings. But eventually that pain makes an introduction. "Hello, kid, my name is pain." When our youngest daughter, Alyssa, was seven, she came running into the house, visibly upset. What you need to understand is that Alyssa has three older siblings, and they are a lot older. When Alyssa was born, Rachel was twelve, Christina was ten, and Josh was six. So her whole life before age seven consisted of her being adored, played with, cuddled, and told how cute she was by her siblings. Well, all that changed on this fateful day. She was playing outside with some neighborhood kids, and Alyssa did something that one of the other kids didn't appreciate. And so one of them told her that she didn't like her anymore. For Alyssa, someone "not liking" her didn't compute. *What does that even mean? Everybody likes me. How can you not like me?* The emotional trauma set in, and the tears began to flow. She ran into the house crying and let us know that someone had told her they didn't like her for the first time. Life got a bit harder that day. The day's lesson was that not everybody likes us, and some people say mean things. Hard lesson.

Watching my kids grow up, experience failure, and make mistakes was painful for me. I wanted them to always be happy, have lots of friends, excel at their sport and musical involvements, succeed at their endeavors, and then meet the perfect boy or girl after high school and never experience a bad breakup. Well, the opposite of the things I just described happened to each one of them. It was hard to see. It was hard to deal with. But these were some of the best things to ever happen to them.

Knowing how to handle human rejection and failure correctly is key to their survival and success as adults.

You have to decide at some point whether you are going to *bail* or *let them fail*. By bail I'm referring to stepping in and bailing them out of a situation that might actually be good for them to go through. I've witnessed parents constantly coming to their children's defense when it would have been best to let them bear the consequences of their actions. Instead of a bailout, maybe they should have considered letting them fail out and learn a valuable life lesson. Teaching our children how to respond to failure in faith and to allow God to use it for their good as they pick themselves up and move forward is critical to their development, confidence, and maturity.

Failure can become an ally and can result in a moment of personal growth that moves us onward toward success from the lessons learned in what I like to call the "big fat failure." We need to help our children understand the powerful dynamics of admitting their mistakes, taking full responsibility for them, and asking forgiveness from those that were affected by their actions. This issue is huge for their future. These learned behaviors and skills will enrich their marriages, advance them in their careers, and make them effective carriers of the gospel, as people respond and are drawn to their humility and transparency.

What is the best life teacher for your children? Your example. When your kids see their mom or dad admit a mistake, take responsibility for it, apologize, and ask for forgiveness from those affected by it, this is an absolutely powerful moment for them. When they see you operate by these principles, they will adopt them in their own lives. As a father, I have done this more times then I want to admit or even think about. But when I made a big mistake and I confessed my error to my kids, told them I was sorry, and asked them to forgive me, a bond was generated between us. Those are powerful moments. Humility creates an atmosphere of deepened love between individuals. The best part came later, when my kids came to me and admitted mistakes they had made. They told me they were sorry and asked me to forgive them. *Wow*—that's a moment! Where did they learn to do that? By watching me and Autumn use the tools of failure and mistakes to create something positive and life-giving, by responding in humility and love.

Tool #5: Unconditional Love

The word *conditional* is defined as "one or more requirements being met." Descriptive adjectives would include "subject to, dependent on, contingent on, based on, determined by, controlled by, tied to." Conditional means works related. If you do this, then I'll do that. Conditional means reciprocal, based on performance. You have to earn it.

Putting the prefix *un* in front *conditional* changes everything. *Un* denotes the absence of the adjectives listed above, in other words, *not* subject to any condition! Unconditional love is wholehearted, unqualified, unreserved, unlimited, unrestricted, unmitigated, unquestioning; it is complete, total, entire, full, absolute, out-and-out, and unequivocal. This is the kind of love that God has toward you and me—amazing love, always-accepting, never-rejecting love. In his letter to the church in Ephesus, Paul describes God's unconditional love in easy-to-understand terms. "And may you have the power to understand, as all God's people should, how wide, how long, how high, and how deep his love is."[3] He uses the terms *wide, long, high,* and *deep* to describe the endlessness of God's love toward his people. Each of those terms describes a vertical or horizontal line with no end. There are no limits or conditions on God's love for his children, as there shouldn't be for ours.

Unconditional love is very hard to produce as parents. In our own broken human limitations, we demand conditions like obedience, respect, and good behavior. When we don't see these in our children, we become angry and disappointed, and we might even go so far as to reject our own children. I've seen this mostly in parents of teenagers who make bad life decisions that challenge the limits of human parental love. What's the answer? Where does a parent find unconditional love when their child's choices or behaviors are so challenging?

I believe it's supernatural. That's right. As God's love for us is supernatural—a love only a perfect God can have—we need to have his supernatural love flowing through us toward our children. How do we get this kind of love for our kids?

Pray for your children every day. It's hard to reject or remain angry at someone we are praying for. We can't hate someone and pray earnestly for them. Prayer softens our hearts toward our children. Prayer helps us feel the same emotions toward our children as God feels. Prayer is what takes the edge off and helps us find peace. In prayer we find the strength to love when it's hard. In prayer we ask God for his intervention in our children's lives. In prayer we find faith to believe our kids will come back and get things right. In prayer we discover protection for our thoughts and feelings, helping us to cope through difficult times. Paul confirms all this when he writes, "Do not be anxious about anything, but in every situation, by prayer and petition, with thanksgiving, present your requests to God. And the peace of God, which transcends all understanding, will guard your hearts and your minds in Christ Jesus."[4] Every parent should have this verse memorized and activated in their daily lives.

Love unconditionally. Loving unconditionally means that no matter what your children do or say, you will love them. The most devastating thing that can happen to your children is to feel your rejection. That is what will send them over the cliff and make matters worse. Showing unconditional love doesn't mean you are never angry or that you refuse to discipline bad behavior. We've talked about that already. But unconditional love is loving them no matter what. Remember—no conditions. It's loving younger children if they throw tantrums, if school grades are bad, or if they act up in church. It's loving teenagers if they date the wrong person, if they fall morally, if they drink or use drugs, if they come out and tell you they are gay or gender confused, and even if they choose to not serve God. The list is endless. And so should your love for them be.

Here is what I've seen over the years. Most kids who stumble and bumble their way through childhood, the teenage, and college years will wake up and come back to God and to reality when they know that, despite all of their bad choices and messes they've made in their lives, they are unconditionally loved by Mom and Dad. Why is that? Because if you still love them after all they put you through, they can believe that God still loves them too. And they'll come back to you and back to God. I've seen so many restoration stories over the years that I can't count them all.

Whenever our kids walked down a wrong path, they knew two things that were true. First, we were disappointed in their decisions. We had open and honest discussions about that. Second, they knew they were loved unconditionally and there was nothing they could do that would break that bond. I made sure that my words and my actions proved that to them. This knowledge enabled them to confess things to us and open their heart to talk with us about their life and the direction they were heading. Today we are very close to all of our children. Unconditional love won the day!

I have a heart for you parents at whatever stage your child is in. Use these tools to help you build a strong relational foundation with your kids. The foundation might crack in a few spots along their way to adulthood, but a few cracks won't destroy a truly strong foundation.

Part Seven

Staying Together

Chapter 20

Back from the Brink

How does a couple remain married for decades? What principles enable them to stick it out and make a marriage work for the long haul? In this final chapter, we want to look at some keys to staying together. Autumn and I have been married over thirty years. Yet I feel less qualified than other couples, who have been married longer then we have, to write about staying together.

So I'm going to tell you a true story about Bob and Stacia. Of all the couples I've met and discussed marriage with over the years, these guys win the prize for being the couple least likely to have stayed together. I share their story because it could be your story. I want to give you hope for your marriage. If God could help Bob and Stacia turn their marriage around, he can do the same for you. I spent an afternoon recording a conversation I had with Bob and Stacia as we sat around their kitchen table on a sunny day in their Northern California home, sipping cold drinks. First, let me give you a brief overview of their relational beginnings, and then we'll pick up the story at the point when the trouble began.

They met in the seventh grade. Bob noticed Stacia running around their junior high school track with her ponytail bouncing and waving behind her. He was smitten by that ponytail and the cute girl it was attached to. They became friends and developed a puppy-love crush on each other. They ended up attending the same high school and also going to the same church. They were actively involved in the church youth group, and it was there they fell in love.

They married in 1962, at the age of nineteen. By the time they were twenty-six, they had two sons and a daughter.

As a husband, Bob was emotionally detached. As a wife, Stacia was broken inside from past sexual abuse. They went to divorce court not once, but twice. Both times, when their marriage seemingly failed, they each had an affair.

Today, they have been married for over fifty years and have never been happier. They have three adult children and seven grandchildren. This is their story from the time when the problems started, about twelve years into their marriage. It begins in Fresno, California.

Bob: In the beginning I thought my role in marriage was to go out and make a living, take care of the family financially, and be there as the "man of the house." In my mind, Stacia's role was to be the housekeeper, the mother; she was to be responsible to take care of all the home-oriented stuff. We came together in the evening, but in my mind I had my role, she had her role, and we just kind of were floating along together. Later, I found out that I was not taking care of her emotional needs. Her emotions were driving me nuts, and I was trying to change them. I wanted her to be emotionally flatlined, like me. That's where my thinking was. I didn't realize it at the time, but she was disconnecting from me emotionally, as I didn't understand her emotional needs. It just so happened that we had friends in the church we were attending at the time, and the husband was much more connected to her emotions than I was. He started paying attention to Stacia and complimenting the great person that she is. It's natural that when you are with someone who is not paying attention to you, and someone else comes along who is paying attention to you, your head swings to the other person.

Stacia: I just transferred any affection I had for Bob to this other man. From one right over to the other.

Bob: I describe my being a bad husband this way. I am blind in one eye. Literally, I can't see out of it. So I have no depth perception. I have very limited perspective. I can't see the world the same as when I could see out of both eyes. When two eyes work together, a person's brain can process the dimensions of a room, for example, and a whole new world opens up. Some people have what is called lazy eye. That's when one eye stops working at seeing properly. The eye gives up trying to see. Lazy eye causes division and limitation when it comes to sight. Two eyes equal togetherness. Two eyes bring two different perspectives working together and an ability to see clearly. Our marriage was like my being able to see out of only one eye. I had my perspective, and that's it. I didn't even know she had a perspective.

Shortly after Stacia's affair with another man, we moved from Fresno to Sacramento. I walked into the bathroom, and here was Stacia in tears. I said rather sternly, "What is wrong with you? You've been in tears ever since we've moved here." She said, "You just don't know what's going on. I left in Fresno a person that I love, and now I'm here with you." I was like … *what just happened here?* It just did not compute with me at all. During this time, my company sent me away to get some training in Chicago. Stacia told me when I left for Chicago, "Don't expect me to be here when you get back." My body hurt so bad from the pain of seeing my marriage crumbling I couldn't stand it. I knew I had to do something but didn't know what to do.

While I was in Chicago, I was able to go see an old male friend. We got together and I spent two hours going on and on about how Stacia did this, and Stacia did that, and I don't deserve this, and on and on it went. Finally, my friend had enough. I'll never forget, he slammed his hand on the table, looked me in the eye, and said, "Bob, your self-righteousness makes me sick" and walked out of the room. It took a while for his comment to sink in, but it did. When I returned to Sacramento after two weeks of job training, I wanted to begin working on our marriage, but Stacia had packed up the kids and moved back to Fresno.

Stacia: While living in Fresno, I had a moment. I saw the man with who I was having an affair with his wife and their three children. And I thought, *What am I doing? I can't do this anymore. I can't take another woman's husband and children away.* Even though I was living in an adulterous relationship and far from God, God still spoke to me by his Spirit, and a moment of clarity came. So I called Bob and asked him if he would be willing to try our marriage again. He got right in the car and came to get us. Even though by now I had filed for divorce.

Bob: I had engaged in an affair myself, and even in the midst of both of us justifying the affairs, God was moving in our hearts. Stacia ended up coming back home, but to be clear, it wasn't for me but for the sake of our children.

At this time, I sought counsel from the pastor who had officiated our wedding. He was a licensed marriage counselor with a PhD in psychology and was now practicing in a town about four hours away from where we lived. He sent us some profiles and assessments to fill out, and I set an appointment to see him. When I arrived at his office, he sat me down and told me that, based on the results of our profiles and assessments, if he knew then what he knew now, he would have never married us. We are that different. That was his final counsel to us. That it will never work and we should end the marriage.

Stacia: But we decided to keep working at it. We changed some things. Bob started to heal from the hurt of my affair.

Bob: I started reading books on marriage. I realized I had been missing meeting her emotional needs and who she was on the inside. I discovered that I can't try to change her, and I needed to appreciate the differences between us. But I still didn't know how this was supposed to work. Unfortunately, I still acted the same way, spoke to her the same way, and ended up hurting her a lot all over again.

Stacia: He showed no empathy or gave any affirmation to me.

Bob: I gave her a lot of negative talk. A lot of sarcasm. In my mind there was still stuff wrong with her. We had moved back to Illinois at this time, and Stacia decided to visit her cousin in Texas. She jumped on a plane and left. At this point, even our pastor in Illinois told us that she needed to leave and have some space away from me. While she was in Texas for about a week, she served me divorce papers again. My reaction this time was, "Okay, that's it; it's over."

(I asked if there was adultery involved again in this second round with the divorce papers. They said yes, on both sides—again).

Stacia: I quickly got a job and established myself in Texas.

Bob: She came back home for the purpose of collecting her things to move to Texas permanently. She met with her lawyer to finalize the divorce. In Illinois there is no waiting period for a divorce to finalize. Once the two parties agree to terms and nobody is contesting anything, the judge can sign the final papers and the divorce is final right then. Well, it just so happens that we were living in northern Illinois, and the attorney lived in southern Illinois, so we were conducting this proceeding on the phone. We went through the whole process of how we were going to divide up the assets, custody of the kids, child-support details, and all that stuff. I was in my office on the conference call, and Stacia was at the house. It just so happened that during the conference call our daughter was in the house with Stacia, practicing her flute in another room. The attorney asked me on the phone, "Bob, are these the conditions (he read them off) that you agree to?". I said yes. The attorney continued, "Stacia, are these the conditions (he read them off) that you agree to?". "Yes," Stacia replied, but then to my surprise, she asked the attorney, "but is it too late to change my mind?" I about fell off my chair.

Stacia: Tell Wil what happened the night before.

Bob: Oh yeah, the night before we had the conference call with the attorney to finalize our divorce, our pastor stopped by my house to check in with me. I told him we were going through with the divorce and there was nothing he could do at this point. He then told me, "I am going to ask the church elders to pray for you guys tonight." I told him, "Go ahead and do what you're going to do, but this marriage is over." So the church pastor and elders prayed for us. Years later, I asked the pastor what they prayed for that night. He said it wasn't what they prayed but how fervently they prayed that our marriage would be healed and restored.

Stacia: Back to the phone call; after all of that, I told the lawyer we weren't going to go through with the divorce. He couldn't believe it. He then wanted to double charge us for his work on our divorce proceedings. Bob and I came together in agreement and both came down on that lawyer. It was the first thing we'd done together as husband and wife in six months (laughter ensues).

Bob: Stacia then told me, "You need to come home, and we need to talk about this." So I'm driving home, and I'm asking myself, *Why is she doing this?* I got home, and she said she couldn't leave her children. She heard our daughter playing the flute, and she came to the realization that she was going to miss seeing the kids grow up through their teenage years. She had a revelation of what our family would become if she left and broke it up. She told me she didn't love me, but she would stay. She said, "I'll live in your home, I'll cook your food, clean your house, wash your clothes. I'll even sleep in the same bed with you, but don't you dare touch me." So that's where we started. We also decided to go back to church. We knew we couldn't isolate ourselves. We also knew we had to humble ourselves, because the people in our church knew about our situation.

Stacia: I felt like I had to wear a big *A* on my chest because of the adultery.

Bob: To the church's credit, they embraced Stacia and loved on her. Just a few weeks after we started attending church again, a couple who was new to the church came up to us and said, "We help couples put their marriage back together and would like to help you." I thought, *Wow, that's God's timing.* So we agreed to meet with them. They were specific and brutally honest, but they taught us how to listen to each other more effectively, and things began to change for us when we carried out the things they were teaching us. I realized I just flat out didn't know how to listen to my wife.

Stacia: In Bob's defense, I wasn't easy to listen to or deal with. I had to deal with many childhood wounds from sexual abuse from age four to my teenage years. So I'm dealing with wounds, and I saw Bob as my knight in shining armor to rescue me. When he didn't, in my mind, I went to other men who I thought could. So when the couple who was helping us assisted me in finding healing for my past wounds, the result was amazing. I learned that you have to get yourself whole. You have to fix your individual brokenness to make your marriage work.

I looked at Bob differently, and our marriage began to change and improve dramatically. When we started the counseling process, I had absolutely no feelings for Bob. I was still emotionally attached to another man. But after about six months of mentoring and coaching and learning how to forgive myself and Bob, something happened. One day he came home from work, and when he was walking through the screen door, I felt love for Bob for the first time in years. As he learned to love me like Paul describes in Ephesians 5, as Christ loves, my "love tank" was full, and all of the sudden, love for him came gushing out of my emotions. And from that point on, we finally began to love each other in a way that's continually brought us closer. It hasn't always been easy. But we learned how to deal with our conflicts in ways that keep us together. We are forever grateful to God and to the couple in our old church that believed in us and helped us through the darkest time in our marriage.

And they are living happily ever after, surrounded by their children and grandchildren. This is an amazing story of relational redemption. In all my years of working with couples, I haven't heard of any that suffered from multiple affairs and divorce court—twice—and still made it. The power of forgiveness and the willingness to do the work necessary to pull their marriage from the brink of divorce is a testimony that should give you hope for your marriage to last.

The last thing I asked Bob and Stacia to share with me was some keys they share with other couples on staying together. Taking what they experienced and shared with me, along with some of my own thoughts, here are six keys to staying together.

Keys to Staying Together

Take responsibility for your own hurts and get well. In Stacia's case it wasn't until she found personal healing for her past abuse that she began to move forward in health and strength and found the ability to love Bob again. We have a saying in our church that goes, "Everybody needs counseling." Reach out and take initiative to get the help you need to get well. Two healed people make a healthy couple.

Get specific instructions on what to do. Bob realized that he was absolutely clueless on what to do to make his marriage better. It wasn't until he and Stacia sat down with a skilled marriage mentor and were told exactly what to do that he began to change. Every spouse needs a specific action plan. I always recommend writing action steps down, taking inventory along the journey, and having someone you are both accountable to as a couple. If you are in a marriage small group, after your meeting go home and write down what you are going to do with what you have learned, and begin to carry it out. If you are seeing a marriage counselor, do the homework that is assigned. Change comes by doing, not by desiring. Desiring is dreaming. Doing is changing.

See the next generation. Stacia awoke to the reality of what divorce would do to their three children while she while she was speaking to the divorce attorney on the phone and at the same time hearing their daughter practicing the flute in her bedroom. The thought shook her to her core, and it literally changed the trajectory of her life. During our interview, tears filled her eyes as she shared the experience and, with emotion in her voice, said, "Where would our kids be if we'd divorced? We now have seven grandchildren, and we would have missed all of the blessings of seeing our family together." Remember that your marriage includes more than just the two of you. I have adult friends who are rocked by the news that after thirty years their parents are splitting up. So, when facing marriage difficulties, look down the generational pipeline a couple decades from now. Imagine what your family would be like if you choose to stay together and work things out, and then what they would be like if you divorce and go your separate ways. Your marriage is bigger than you.

Get your ego out of the way. It takes humility to admit your faults in your marriage. It's very difficult to focus on your weaknesses and the things you need to change instead of finger pointing and criticizing your spouse and his or her faults. Remember that you are half of the problem. You need to fix some stuff. You can't change your spouse, but you can change yourself. You have to lay pride down and take a modest position of humility in order to build up something strong.

Have a lot of humor. Learning to laugh at yourself is one of life's greatest gifts. Learning to laugh with each other is even better. Notice I said *with* each other, not *at* each other. Big difference. I often encourage couples in counseling to lighten up and enjoy life more with each other. I suggest they watch a funny movie together or take a walk and don't allow themselves to talk about anything negative. "There is a time to weep and a time to laugh."[1] Many couples allow themselves to become so miserable that they only make time to weep and never time to laugh. I'm always amazed, when I counsel couples to make time and go out on a date, or away for the weekend and do something fun, that the reaction is one of shock, as if they've never heard of the concept before. Somewhere along the continuum of their marriage, they forgot how to have fun and how to laugh. Bob and Stacia have a horrible history of pain, rejection, hurt, adultery, and sexual abuse. But if you could listen to the interview recording, you'd hear them laughing about how miserable their life was. They now joke about how they shouldn't be together and that they did everything possible to ruin their marriage. It's the joy of the Lord bursting through their hearts because of what's transpired in their marriage. Don't forget to laugh.

Remember that every part of your life flows into your marriage. Bob was remembering how important his work was to him.

His identity was found in career success, and because of that he didn't invest in his marriage. As a young husband, he thought his work was separate from his marriage. Stacia, on the other hand, developed relationships with men besides Bob, which started off harmlessly but developed into destructive relationships resulting in adultery. Work, outside relationships, activities, and even church involvement all flow into and have an effect on your marriage. It's all one and the same. It's called life. When a friend of mine played on three different softball teams simultaneously, those softball teams flowed into his marriage. And it wasn't a home run, for sure. He almost lost his marriage because of softball. When old boyfriends and girlfriends reach out on Facebook and fire up the friendship again, that is going to flow into their marriages. When a co-worker of the opposite sex texts you a message that isn't professional or work related, and maybe a little flirty, that is going to flow into your marriage. Everything in your life starts with the strength of your marriage and works its way out. When your marriage is together, all other parts of your life come together. When all the other parts of your life aren't together, then your marriage will suffer. So get it together! And by all means, stay together.

I hope that this book helps you find the togetherness you're looking for in marriage. There is nothing like it when it's working. Finding your togetherness groove is the greatest discovery you can experience. And the best part is that you will experience it *together*!

Endnotes

Introduction

[1] *Science of Longtime Couples Who Die Together* by Melissa Dahl, *NYMAG. com*, November 19, 2015. http://nymag.com/scienceofus/2015/11/science-of-longtime-couples-who-die-together.html

[2] *A Final Embrace* by Rebecca Perring, *Express.uk.co.*, July 3, 2015. http://www.express.co.uk/news/world/588638/Couple-dying-embrace-die-together-married-75-years

Chapter One

[1] Genesis 3:8–19

Chapter Two

[1] As referenced by Toni Ridgaway in the online article, *Cohabitation Is New Normal for Young Families*, April 4, 2012. http://www.churchleaders.com/pastors/pastor-articles/166635-cohabitation-is-new-normal-for-young-families,

[2] *The New Unmarried Moms*, by Kay Hymowitz, W. Bradford Wilcox and Kelleen Kay, March 15, 2013. http://www.wsj.com/articles/SB1000142412 7887323826704578356494206134184

[3] Andrew J. Cherlin, *The Marriage-Go-Round: The State of Marriage and The Family in America Today* (New York, NY; Knopf Publishing 2009) 156.

[4] Timothy Keller, *The Meaning of Marriage: Facing the Complexities of Commitment with the Wisdom of God* (New York, NY; Penguin Group 2011. Kindle Edition). 23.

[5] *Pastors: That Divorce Stat You Quoted Is Probably Wrong* by Ed Stetzer, http://www.churchleaders.com/pastors/pastor-articles/163047-pastors-that-divorce-stat-you-quoted-is-probably-wrong.html

[6] *The Social Costs of Abandoning the Meaning of Marriage*, Ryan T. Anderson, September 19, 2013. http://www.heritage.org/research/reports/2013/09/the-social-costs-of-abandoning-the-meaning-of-marriage.

Chapter Three

[1] Andreas J. Kostenberger, with David Jones, *God, Marriage, and Family: Rebuilding the Biblical Foundation*, second edition (Wheaton, Ill; Crossway2010). 77–78.

[2] Matthew 19:6, Proverbs 2:16–17, Malachi 2:14–16

[3] Genesis 2:22

[4] Genesis 2:23–25, 1 Corinthians 7:3–4

[5] Ephesians 5:25–30

[6] Ephesians 5:22

[7] Sean McDowell; John Stonestreet, *Same-Sex Marriage: A Thoughtful Approach to God's Design for Marriage* (Grand Rapids, MI; Baker Publishing Group. Kindle Edition 2014). 33.

[8] Genesis 2:24

[9] Genesis 2:18

[10] *The Horrible Psychology of Solitary Confinement*, by Brandon Keim, July 13, 2013. http://www.wired.com/2013/07/solitary-confinement-2.

[11] Genesis 1:28

Chapter Five

[1] Matthew 15:4–8; 19:19; Mark 7:6,10; 10:19; Luke 18:20; Ephesians 6:2; 1 Timothy 5:3; 1 Peter 2:17

[2] Matthew 27:9

³ John 5:23

⁴ Dr. Gary Chapman, *The 5 Love Languages* (Chicago, Ill; Northfield Publishing 1992). 51.

⁵ 1 Peter 5:6–7 ESV

Chapter Six

¹ Ephesians 5:33b

Chapter Eleven

¹ *Holman Illustrated Bible Dictionary*, (Nashville, TN: Holman Bible Publishers, 2003).

² Drs. Les and Leslie Parrott, *The Good Fight*, (Brentwood, TN; Worthy Publishing, 2013). 75.

Chapter Twelve

¹ *VR Porn Is Here and Its Scary How Realistic It Is,* by Raymond Wong, January 8, 2016. http://mashable.com/2016/01/08/naughty-america-vr-porn-experience/#d6bVyS7Qemqd

² *By 2025, Sexbots Will Be Commonplace*, by Sebastian Anthony, August 14, 2014. http://www.extremetech.com/extreme/188047-by-2025-sexbots-will-be-commonplace-which-is-just-fine-as-well-all-be-unemployed-and-bored-thanks-to-robots-stealing-our-jobs

³ http://dailyreadlist.com/article/how-technology-will-change-the-way-we-have-sex-27

⁴ Laura Sessions Stepp. *Unhooked: How Young Women Pursue Sex, Delay Love and Lose at Both* (New York, NY; Riverhead Books, Kindle Edition, 2007). Location 185.

⁵ Ibid.

⁶ Michael Kimmel, *Guyland*, (HarperCollins ebooks, Kindle Edition, 2009). 192.

⁷ According to the Kinsey Institute, California State University

[8] *The Ashley Madison Hack,* by CNNMONEY Staff, August 24, 2015. http://money.cnn.com/2015/08/24/technology/ashley-madison-hack-in-2-minutes/index.html

[9] Larry Crabb, *The Marriage Builder: Creating True Oneness to Transform Your Marriage.* (Grand Rapids, MI; Zondervan, Kindle Edition, 2013). Location 1509.

Chapter Thirteen

[1] Timothy Keller, *The Meaning of Marriage: Facing the Complexities of Commitment with the Wisdom of God* (New York, NY; Penguin Publishing Group, Kindle Edition, 2011). 215.

Chapter Sixteen

[1] *Institution of the Family Being Eroded,* by Joel Kotkin, *Orange County Register,* July 12, 2015. http://www.ocregister.com/articles/families-671094-children-social.html

Chapter Eighteen

[1] Ephesians 6:1–3

[2] M. H. Manser, *Dictionary of Bible Themes: The Accessible and Comprehensive Tool for Topical Studies.* (London: Martin Manser, 2009).

[3] John 10:10

Chapter Nineteen

[1] Hebrews 12:5–11

[2] *The 42 Countries That Have Banned Corporeal Punishment,* November 20, 2014. http://untribune.com/42-countries-banned-corporal-punishment/

[3] Ephesians 3:18, New Living Translation

[4] Philippians 4:6–7

Chapter Twenty

[1] Ecclesiastes 3:4

Printed in the United States
By Bookmasters